Good teaching and learning: pupils and teachers speak

Good teaching and learning: pupils and teachers speak

Colin Morgan and Glyn Morris

Open University Press
Buckingham · Philadelphia

Open University Press
Celtic Court
22 Ballmoor
Buckingham
MK18 1XW

email: enquiries@openup.co.uk
world wide web: http://www.openup.co.uk

and
325 Chestnut Street
Philadelphia, PA 19106, USA

First Published 1999

A catalogue record of this book is available from the British Library

ISBN   0 335 20262 4 (pb)   0 335 20263 2 (hb)

Library of Congress Cataloging-in-Publication Data
Morgan, Colin.
     Good teaching and learning : pupils and teachers speak/Colin
Morgan and Glyn Morris.
       p.   cm.
     Includes bibliographical references (p. 160) and index.
     ISBN 0–335–20263–2 (hardcover). – ISBN 0–335–20262–4 (pbk.)
     1. High school teaching–Great Britain–Evaluation–Case studies.
2. Learning–Evaluation–Case studies.   3. Teachers–Self-rating of–
Great Britain–Case studies.   4. Education and state–Great
Britain–Case studies.   5. Comprehensive high schools–Wales–Case
studies.   I. Morris, Glyn, 1932–   . II. Title.
LB1737.G7M67   1998
373.1102–dc21   98–18442
                                                                        CIP

Typeset by Graphicraft Limited, Hong Kong
Printed in Great Britain by Biddles Ltd, Guildford and King's Lynn

Contents

Acknowledgements

A considerable number of people have enabled and encouraged the development of this project. The research on which this book is based could not have been carried out without the support of the headteachers and members of the teaching staff in the schools concerned. We cannot name them, but we do thank them warmly for the access and friendly hospitality they gave us. We thank also our colleagues from the Open University in Wales: Cenmyr Thomas, a constant source of help, who contributed to the data collection in the schools; and Lesley Richards, who supplied a stream of information about current policy requirements for teachers. In the initial stage of the project, the contribution of Glyn Rogers, now of University of Wales, Cardiff, was invaluable. Financial assistance for the work of this project was provided by the Centre for Curriculum and Teaching Studies in the School of Education of the Open University, and we thank colleagues there for their encouragement, and particularly Bob McCormick.

List of tables and figure

Tables

Figure

1 | Introduction: the policy background, the research and the contents of this book

This book is about the participants' views of learning and teaching in British comprehensive schools. It derives from the spoken views of pupils and teachers collected in ten schools over a period of five years in the mid-1990s, a time when government was dramatically changing the whole pattern of control of state provided education.

The background policy context

Beginning in the 1980s, public policy for education had seen increasing system intervention by government, by way of both much legislation and frequent exhortation declaredly aimed at securing greater effectiveness from its schools. This represented a significant shift from the previous three-quarters of a century, generally characterized as a national system locally administered. For the best part of a century following the Industrial Revolution, the state schools could be seen in broad terms to have provided a 20 per cent elite for employment in various leadership roles and a similar minority of technicians, craftsmen and clerical workers to make, repair and service the machines or clerk the commerce of Britain and its Empire. Priorities in public education were to change dramatically, however, in response to the 'global economy' and 'information technology' revolutions which became evident by the 1980s; the many instead of the few henceforth needed to be maximally educated, and the link between public educational provision and economic performance strengthened.

Whereas in past decades an essentially passive compliant labour force equipped with little more than the basic three Rs had been required, the 'information society' demands maximum cognitive achievement together with creative and social skills from all its children if the country is to compete successfully in a global economy. Hence, in both the UK and many other countries since the early 1980s, public policy for education has seen greater prescription of the curriculum and the introduction of national testing, more financial control devolved to the individual school in parallel with explicit and rigorous external inspection, and a marked focus generally on the performance of schools.

As the 1990s proceeded, and irrespective of which political party was in power, the target of government intervention in the control of schools changed from the *system to the classroom* and, in the process, focused upon the issue of good and bad teaching, together with an increased readiness to grapple with the problem of 'bad teachers'. In short, having addressed structural issues of accountability and control as a response to the global changes, the concern of government in the UK has now moved to individual pupils' learning achievement and the effectiveness of their teachers. It is to this topic that the voices of the secondary school pupils and teachers described in this book relate, for the aim of the research which this book reports was to capture the views of pupils and teachers on what they defined as *quality* in learning and teaching.

In the 1980s, we were both very involved in the evaluation of the Technical and Vocational Education Initiative (TVEI) in eighteen schools across several local education authorities (LEAs), and had found that secondary school pupils of whatever age were very observant about their school experience and capable of analytical and constructive comments when we interviewed them. We found, though, that their right to express views on school matters was not everywhere conceded by school leaders, or, when it was, the views they had expressed were not necessarily heeded in all schools. Their voices *were* heard when TVEI evaluation reports were considered at consortium level or even at LEA meetings to consider our findings. We were thus convinced that pupils have the potential to play an effective part in the guiding of policy. We also spoke with many teachers at the time, and always found them to be positive in response to our enquiries. Even though they often said that they had arrived at our interview rooms not really 'knowing what it was all about or what to expect', by the end of the conversation they invariably indicated that they had enjoyed the opportunity to talk about their work and concerns on a one-to-one basis. The TVEI experience had convinced us that much can be learned from listening to the key actors on the classroom stage.

It is not unusual for the experience and views of teachers on learning and teaching effectiveness to find a place in publications, and over recent years there have been a range of significant books, among them Cullingford (1995), Kyriacou (1991) and Wragg (1984). In contrast, the voice of pupils is markedly less evident in research and publication, and the legitimacy of pupils to comment on their classroom experience on teaching, or on teachers, still has something of a shadowy status.

The value and legitimacy of pupil perspectives

When the opportunities came along for us to do research in schools about the quality of learning and teaching, we saw it as important to give greater weight in the research design to the contribution of the pupil perspective. The pupils were to be our key respondent group, and we asked them more questions on our research topic and interviewed more of them than we did of the teachers, because their views have been, and still are, relatively neglected. Over a decade ago Beynon (1985: 188) wrote that although

> more attention was being paid to pupils' perspectives (how they view schooling and teachers and how they react, what they see as 'ideal', 'good' and 'bad' etc.) . . . it still remains a comparatively neglected topic, even in the work of those who have paid attention to pupil perspectives . . . Indeed, the pupil role has too often been presented as merely conforming to, or rejecting of, school demands.

Similar judgements were still being expressed as recently as 1993 by Lang, who had himself made important research contributions on pupil perceptions of pastoral care. Regarding the voices of pupils more generally, however, he wrote: 'the neglect of student perspectives on schooling . . . has been a persistent concern over many years . . . in spite of the fact that where student perspectives were investigated the results were often extremely significant, as in the case of Hargreaves' early classic work *Social Relations in a Secondary School* (1967) and Willis' later influential book *Learning to Labour* (1980)' (Lang 1993: 308). What research has not yet provided, he asserted, 'is the kind of information which might allow schools and teachers to do better. To do this, research involving discussion with students and perhaps comparing student and teacher views is needed' (Lang 1993: 312).

Since Lang's correct judgement of need – in our view – there has been the impressive response of Jean Rudduck (1996) and colleagues by way of the pioneering study *School Improvement: What Can Pupils Tell Us?*, which was based on more than 900 pupil interviews, mainly carried out in three schools over four years. The standpoint of Rudduck and colleagues is that the pupil perspective is insufficiently valued and that it is an important input for policies seeking greater effectiveness:

> Our argument in this book is that what pupils say about teaching, learning and schooling is not only worth listening to but provides an important – perhaps the most important – foundation for thinking about ways of improving schools. Our broad summary of what pupils have told us in interview is that whilst teachers are for the most part supportive, stimulating and selfless in the hours they put in to help young people, the conditions of learning that are common across secondary schools do not adequately take account of the social maturity of young people.
>
> (Rudduck 1996: 1)

This has been our experience too, and we heartily endorse this view. It was exactly for these kinds of reasons that we had resolved to collect pupil views on their learning and teaching, and to compare them with parallel teacher perspectives. Whereas the landmark book of Rudduck draws on four linked studies and deals with all aspects of pupils making their way through secondary school, the topic areas we present in this book are more restricted. They are essentially confined to the detail of classroom matters, classroom relations, methods and organization, the enhancers and inhibitors of learning etc. The work of Rudduck and colleagues covers the whole landscape of pupils' experience of secondary schooling, whereas ours is more a portrait than a landscape, in that it is focused on but one of a school's arenas. We intend that it might bring on to the stage of policy discussion the whole issue of the contribution of pupil voices, alongside those of teachers, to improving the quality of classroom teaching and learning.

The legitimacy of taking pupil views into account has been challenged by some headteachers ever since early work in discovering pupil perspectives (Meighan 1977), and we have ourselves experienced such objections before and after the event of interviewing pupils. Apart from the reticence of some to take pupil opinion seriously that we experienced in our TVEI evaluation studies, most recently, in one of the ten schools of this study (School B, Table 1.1) we were unable, after completing the pupil interviews, to fulfil the interviewing of a selection of their teachers. The reaction by the head and school's senior management was adverse to the report we returned to them, which contained verbatim references to what the pupils had said regarding certain areas of school policy they had asked us to investigate. On being given the feedback messages, they said that, in essence, they did not see the children as competent to judge the behaviour of adults. Such a viewpoint has not, of course, kept pace with science, quite apart from the self-evident value of the range of researches – in addition to Lang and Rudduck – which invoke pupils' perspectives (Mishra 1980; Phelan *et al.* 1992; Cooper 1993; Cooper and McIntyre 1995). The plain fact is that there are now also many research studies that have used rigorous experimental methods to demonstrate that pupils are clearly competent to perceive teachers' behaviours accurately, and are able to interpret their intent correctly (for example, see Babad *et al.* 1991, which cites a whole raft of literature to this effect).

All of this is not to suggest that teachers' views have had a great deal of notice taken of them. There has probably been a bit more research than has been the case for pupil perspectives, but government in its several forms has rarely sought the views of classroom teachers.

The research background to this book

This book derives from research carried out in ten comprehensive schools across the whole of the south of Wales between 1992 and 1997. We had arranged to be in these schools on the *quid pro quo* basis that we could collect information to do with the quality of learning and teaching in return for our carrying out surveys of topics requested by the schools themselves. Across the ten schools, these surveys have covered: the extent of bullying; what should be done about bullying; the support teachers receive from senior management; the quality of the school environment; how the homework policy is working and what changes pupils would make; uniform; working of the supported self-learning scheme; working of the homework diary; reasons for differential achievement of boys and girls; school policy on order and discipline; evaluation of pupil individual action plans; and extending achievements by the middle ability range.

While there was a distinctive purpose to our visits to each of the schools, we were also at one and the same time conducting a core project which we called 'the quality of learning project', where we asked a common set of questions to pupils and teachers. Because of other research contacts in earlier years, or because one or the other of us had taught a member of the senior management team on postgraduate courses, in each of these ten schools we were confident that we were in good standing to request access for our 'quality of learning' topic interests, while at the same time offering to provide the school with information on concerns of its choosing. This *quid pro quo* meant, then, that the school received a written report on a topic of policy concern to itself at the time, while we could find out how the prime participants – the pupils and teachers – defined 'good teaching' and what they perceived as constituting 'good learning experiences'. Our 'quality of learning' study, and hence eventually this book, derives from research work done on the back of investigating other topics.

In all the schools we conducted our 'quality of learning' researches by way of one-to-one interviews mainly using open-ended questions with *representative* samples of pupils and *opportunity* samples of teachers. We therefore imposed no prior categorizations and did not assume any relationships to or explanations of the topic areas of teaching and learning in which we were interested. What we were to find out has not come from answers to preset question options, but was derived by analysing the themes and meanings embedded in the answers which the pupil and teacher respondents themselves gave. While our research approach is essentially qualitative, we are always concerned to demonstrate by quantification, wherever possible, the representativeness and frequency of the perspectives revealed. Hence, this book contains a good many tables which convey the frequency and representativeness of the meanings or 'constructs' expressed by our pupil and teacher interviewees. In addition to these qualitative approaches, we sometimes used written survey instruments, as will become evident.

The schools where we interviewed

The ten comprehensive schools which provided the information for this book are spread out geographically in the south of Wales, with a distance of about one hundred miles between those furthest apart. As Table 1.1

Table 1.1 The ten schools

School	Description	Number on roll	Pupil interviews	Teacher interviews	Year groups covered
A (LEA 1)	Commuter suburb housing estate comprehensive	1,200	12	13	7 to 9 and 11 to 13
B (LEA 2)	Mixed urban/rural comprehensive	700	36	0	7 to 13
C (LEA 3)	Large council housing estate urban comprehensive	1,000	19	15	7 to 11
D (LEA 2)	Wholly rural comprehensive	600	20	15	7 to 10 and 12
E (LEA 4)	Affluent city comprehensive	1,400	16	16	7 to 10
F (LEA 2)	Coastal town comprehensive	1,450	18	14	7 to 11
G (LEA 5)	Balanced social class city fringe comprehensive	970	28	11	7 to 11
H (LEA 3)	Urban working-class comprehensive	1,130	19	14	7 to 11
I (LEA 1)	'Rough' large housing estate comprehensive	1,140	19	20	7 to 11
J (LEA 5)	Small town with surrounding villages comprehensive	950	20	15	7 to 11
Totals		10,480	207	133	7 year groups

shows, they, like comprehensive schools everywhere, are characterized by socially and geographically different catchment areas, and some are 'polar' contrasts to each other. School D, for example, serves a scattered population in a totally rural area, whereas school H draws all its children from a quite densely populated wholly urban area; school E has a very affluent catchment area, with the largest proportion of children from professional parents, whereas school I, in contrast, draws its children from the roughest of housing estates with a high incidence of social problems. In between these polarities the other six schools represent the sort of social mixes or locations which exist for comprehensive schools across England and Wales.

While Wales is a bilingual part of the United Kingdom, and as a consequence has a growing number of comprehensive schools which teach at least half the National Curriculum subjects through the minority language, none of these is represented in the schools shown in Table 1.1. All the schools which provided the research data on which this book is based are English-medium comprehensive schools, and are no different in organization or structure from any we have both worked in across England.

All the schools were of course guaranteed institutional anonymity in our use of the information we obtained, as also were the individual pupils and teachers interviewed. We presented to these schools the purpose of our research interviewing in terms of a formal written contract statement, the key elements of which were:

- *Purpose of this interview.* This interview forms part of our collecting information regarding the classroom work of pupils and teachers and may throw light on issues connected with the quality of learning and teaching in schools generally.
- *Ethics and scope of this interview.* This interview is not concerned in any way with the appraisal of particular individuals or the assessment of the work of any department in your school. The project does not focus on individual people or, indeed, on any individual school *per se*, as the essential purpose of the project is to bring together information which may illuminate issues of quality across schools generally.
- *Rules of the interview – confidentiality and non-attribution.* No information given by you in answers to questions during this interview will be attributed to you; nor will any information deriving from your answers to questions be presented in any report in such a way that could identify you as the source of any statement. The intention is that the information obtained from this and other interviews will be aggregated for analysis and, if developed into any report material, would be presented in positive ways intended to be of help to teachers generally.

We did not provide the schools with any schedules of our interview questions prior to the visits, though if asked, we indicated orally the topics we would be covering. In these ten schools all told, we carried out nearly 350 interviews, and on no occasion was any objection raised about any question asked.

The pupils interviewed

Table 1.1 gives the total number of pupils we met in interview in each of the ten schools, and the numbers vary from school to school. We had in fact intended there to be a standard number and had made the following standard request to all the schools.

Pupil interviewees: what are we looking for?

Pupils. From each of Years 7 to 11, we would wish to interview (about 20–25 minutes each) four pupils from each year, so as to give a grand total of 20 for the school as a whole. It does not matter who the pupils are, save that there should be an equal balance of boys and girls from each year group, and that they should reflect the ability range in respect of school performance, with about 25 per cent of them pupils teachers would designate as 'upper ability' and another 25 per cent those teachers would designate as 'lower ability'.

Another feature we would like to have represented in the pupils we interview would be the proportion of the year group who have free school meals. Hence, to take, for example, Year 7 (and assuming that there are 44 per cent free meals for the year group population as a whole), we would wish to receive as interviewees from Year 7 pupils the following pattern: two girls and two boys; two pupils in middle ability group, one pupil in upper and one pupil in the lower ability groups; any two of the above to be of free school meal status.

Organizational arrangements

The two interviewers would need separate rooms for confidentiality, though little overall space is required, just sufficient for a table and two chairs. Teachers and pupils should be told that the interviews are part of a larger survey of schools concerned with a project on pupil learning, and that the interviews imply no assessment of any individual or school involved whatsoever, as the views of individuals, whether teachers or pupils, are being sought solely to derive a larger picture concerned with pupil learning and classroom practices.

Our original design had therefore intended a standard stratified sample total of 20 pupils per school on the basis of interviewing four pupils per year group for Years 7 to 11. We had found in the past that stratifying by gender, ability and age allowed us to draw out relationships from the data which would otherwise be hidden, as well as giving best representativeness with the minimum of interviews. In the event, however, several things happened to modify the total number of pupils we actually interviewed in each of the ten schools: sometimes a certain year group was not available; sometimes the individual school thought it important to include some pupils from Years 12 and 13. For three of the ten schools where twenty

Table 1.2 The pupils interviewed in the ten schools by gender and ability group

	Upper ability		Middle ability		Lower ability		Totals
	Boys	Girls	Boys	Girls	Boys	Girls	
	21	37	52	42	32	23	207
Totals by ability category	58(28%)		94(45%)		55(27%)		207(100%)

pupils had been scheduled to meet us, one failed to show on the day; hence there is the apparently odd-looking total of nineteen. In some cases schools interpreted the request differently from what we had intended, and had arranged more pupil interviewees than we had requested, but when we turned up we took what they had arranged anyway. A consequence of the differing number of respondents from the schools, whether pupils or teachers, is that we have standardized for group size by using percentages in the later tables where we present the various categories of response to particular perspectives.

We found it a pleasure meeting the pupils, who, save for a very small number from whom obtaining answers was like pulling teeth, were all very ready to talk. We did not really meet what Beynon (1985) has described as 'oppositional' pupils, so whether we were shielded from the really hard cases by the school's choice we do not know. Nevertheless, the out-turn position for most schools, and certainly for the schools as a whole (Tables 1.2 and 1.3), was one where we had the gender and ability balances which were required to satisfy representation of these key profile factors of the pupil populations as a whole. We had aimed to interview 25 per cent lower and upper ability pupils, and as Table 1.2 shows, we achieved out-turns of 28 per cent and 27 per cent respectively. We had wanted an equal balance of girl and boy interviewees, and we almost exactly achieved this, having interviewed, from the total of 207 pupils, 105 boys or 50.73 per cent and 102 girls or 49.27 per cent. However, it will be noted from Table 1.2 that the gender balances of the ability sub-groups we received were not equal. Girls were more likely to be selected for the upper ability categorization and boys for the lower.

Regarding representation from year groups, our research design had been to interview in each school equal numbers of pupils from Years 7 to 11, but Year 11 proved to be a problem. It turned out that, in the case of three of the ten schools, our visits coincided with the time when Year 11 pupils were preoccupied with approaching examinations or had completed them. Hence, as shown in Table 1.3, whereas for each of the first four statutory years of secondary schooling we interviewed virtually the same numbers of pupils across the schools, for Year 11 we achieved only about

Table 1.3 The pupils interviewed in the ten schools by year group

Year 7	Year 8	Year 9	Year 10	Year 11	Year 12	Year 13	Total
40	42	42	41	25	11	6	207

60 per cent of our target number of interviewees, but there was a compensation in that the schools which were unable to supply Year 11 pupils sent some Year 12 and 13 pupils instead. What became subsequently clear was that the pattern of data from Years 11, 12 and 13 pupils did not in the event differ from the other data.

The teacher interviewees

Our interviews with the 133 teachers took place in nine out of the ten schools, and the numbers we received varied from eleven in school G to twenty in school J, with about fifteen being the usual number. We had made a similar standard request to each of the schools regarding our requirements for teacher interviewees. We had written as follows. 'Teachers: if possible we would like to talk for about 20–25 minutes with about 14–16 teachers across the subject range, and with varying lengths of teaching experience, who teach pupils in Years 7–11.'

We could not make a more precise request in terms of a strict sample reflecting gender balance, subjects taught or age range, for who would be available would be dependent on individual teaching timetables and the demands in the particular school on the day. The best that could be achieved would be that the teachers who could be free to meet us would be reasonably representative in respect of gender, length of teaching service and range of subjects taught to the pupils in these schools.

Table 1.4 shows the distribution of these in respect of gender and length of service. So that we could later assess whether there were any different response patterns linked with the length of service of teachers, we allocated them to the three 'length of teaching service' categories shown in Table 1.4. As it happened to turn out, the three categories in terms of length of service were fairly evenly matched. We have no way of knowing whether the distribution shown in Table 1.4 is representative of all the teachers in these schools or not. Our impression was that we received a few percentage more in the 'younger' service group than would be the case for the population as a whole. In terms of gender, of the 133 teacher interviewees there were 71 (or 53 per cent) males and 62 (or 47 per cent females), and again we do not know how representative this would be of the staff of these ten schools as a whole. But the out-turn gender balance was such that we could securely search for any response patterns which might be significantly related to gender.

Table 1.4 The teacher interviewees by gender and length of service

Length of service category	1 to 10 years		Between 11 and 20 years		Over 20 years		Totals
	Female	Male	Female	Male	Female	Male	
	28	23	25	18	18	21	133
Totals	51(38.3%)		43(32.3%)		39(29.3%)		

In Table 1.5 we show, by way of our own (perhaps somewhat arbitrary) subject groupings, the actual out-turn distribution on the basis of the main subject the teacher interviewees said they taught when we met them. On the face of it, it looks to be a reasonably valid reflection of what exists for the population of teachers as a whole in comprehensive schools. In fact, because the schools wanted reliable feedback on the survey topics of their choosing, there was every incentive for them to secure for us a reasonable cross-section of their teaching staff. In some cases, we were able after our visits to compare staff lists with the profile of those actually interviewed, and there was every indication that we had received broadly representative groups of interviewees in terms of gender and subjects taught.

'Learning and teaching quality' and the questions we asked the pupils and teachers

While it may be self-evident that the quality of what exactly happens in the classrooms is the crucial factor governing the achievements of the child and school as a whole, what constitutes 'good' learning or a 'good' or 'bad' teacher is still to be made explicit in any detailed way, though it is true that the Teacher Training Agency and Ofsted have set out standards and criteria regarding what they regard as satisfactory for the classroom and training standards to be met by new teachers, and we shall consider their views in the light of our findings in our concluding chapter.

We take the view, however, that there would probably be general agreement that, in the history of British teachers, teaching and education discussion generally, there has been relatively little professional discussion of classroom pedagogy, but much concern with teachers' autonomy, professional status or desired social role in redressing social inequalities. The whole topic of the appropriate pedagogy, how to enhance classroom learning and the nature of the 'skills sets' needed by teachers for the twenty-first century is now very much on the agenda. Our view is that the key actors, the pupils and teachers, should legitimately have a major contributory role

Table 1.5 The teacher interviewees by subjects taught across the ten schools

Subject group	Arts	Maths /science	Social science	Languages	Fine and performing arts	Technology	Physical education	Others	Totals
Examples	English, history, RE	Physics, chemistry, biology, combined sciences	Economics, geography	French, German, Welsh	Art, drama, music	CDT, computing	PE	Business studies, special needs, SMT	
A	3	5	0	3	0	0	0	2	13
B	–	–	–	–	–	–	–	–	0
C	3	7	2	1	1	1	0	0	15
D	3	4	1	2	0	0	2	3	15
E	2	5	1	3	2	1	1	1	16
F	2	5	2	3	2	0	0	0	14
G	1	4	3	1	1	1	0	0	11
H	2	2	0	4	3	2	0	1	14
I	9	2	1	2	1	3	1	1	20
J	4	2	0	2	1	1	2	3	15
Total	29	36	10	21	11	9	6	11	133

to play in this discussion. Hence, we framed a common core set of questions intended to reveal what they think about the 'quality of learning and teaching' issues.

The same questions were to be asked in all ten schools irrespective of the particular school-requested topic being investigated. An important and overarching concern behind our framing of the question schedule was the extent to which pupil and teacher perspectives on classroom practice were in harmony or discord. In the latter case, we intended to pick out and highlight critical factors which seemed to be of significance. Principally, it was intended, however, that responses to these common core questions might provide policy resource for enhancing classroom learning as well as saying something about the whole area of teacher competences.

The core questions asked in the schools

The questions we asked are shown in Table 1.6. The italic type in the questions conveys the particular emphases we imparted to the questions. We need to indicate here that the pupils, in addition to the four questions

Table 1.6 The questions asked

Questions to pupils	*Questions to teachers*
1 Do you think you *learn more* in some lessons than others? (If answer is YES) What makes *the difference* between lessons where you learn a lot and those where you don't learn much?	1 To what do you attribute *differences in the rate at which pupils learn* – that some pupils learn better than others?
2 Do you think that some of your teachers are *better as teachers* than others? (If answer is YES) What makes some teachers *better* than others?	2 We hear a lot about traditional and progressive methods of teaching. Do you yourself have an *identifiable style* of teaching and if so, how would you categorize your style of classroom teaching?
3 Think of one of your *best* lessons since you have been at this school. What made it a good lesson for you?	3 Think of *a specially good lesson* that you have given recently – when you came from the classroom and thought *that lesson went excellently*. What were the factors that contributed to it being a good one?
4 Think of one of your *worst* lessons since you have been at this school. What made it a bad lesson for you?	

set out above, were also asked to complete a 'self-completion form' of several items, including a rating matrix of eleven items that required a scale response to four options from 'not important' to 'very important' on the topic of: 'The lessons in which I learn most are those where . . .'. We shall discuss the findings from this in Chapter 4. There were, of course, additional questions on this topic area which we would have liked to have asked, but we were constrained by the time available for the interviewees, especially as we had to cover the individual school's subject of investigation. We therefore had to be content that the answers to the core questions would illuminate teaching and learning issues, and reveal insights from the previously relatively neglected pupil perspective.

While the core of our research approaches is therefore essentially *qualitative*, in that we are crucially concerned to discover the meanings that participants attach to their behaviour, how they interpret situations and what their perspectives are, we hold to an eclectic and open attitude to research methods, and, as already indicated, will sometimes use highly structured paper and pencil questionnaires alongside interviewing. In fact, we believe, like some other researchers (for example, Bird 1985), that the linking of qualitative and quantitative data can reveal important pay-offs. Hence, we find benefit in quantifying the categories of meanings induced from the qualitative data, and in looking for statistical relationships between particular perspectives and defined subsets of respondents.

Table 1.7 Format of tables in text: illustration 1

Main construct categories	% response in category*
Main construct I	54
Main construct II	37
Main construct III	9
Total	100

* The percentages here are for illustration purposes only

The consequence of this approach for this book is that we shall be presenting a good many tables to convey the intensity and frequency of the perspectives and meanings we have drawn from the answers given by pupils and teachers to our questions. We shall be using a common framework to the pattern of tables set out in the text. That is, for the particular question put, the *main construct categories*, or 'meaning perspectives', deriving from our analysis of the interview responses will be shown first, and after some comment, each of these main constructs will be further explored through a consideration of the respective *subconstructs*, or submeaning categories which make up the main category. For example there will be a main table in the format shown in Table 1.7.

After discussion of the main table, with its various main categories of response, each of the main constructs will be considered in respect of its subunits, so that to take 'main construct I', for example, the 54 per cent of

Table 1.8 Format of tables in text: illustration 2

The subcategories of response	% responses
Subconstruct I	25
Subconstruct II	16
Subconstruct III	13
Total mean % response to subcategory	54

responses allocated to it will be subsequently distributed and described in the relevant subcategories as set out in Table 1.8.

The reader will find tables following these patterns in Chapters 2, 3, 4, 5 and 6. In addition to tables along these lines, we also show, wherever possible in table format, the quantified responses across schools, so as to convey the extent to which particular perspectives are consistent across schools of widely different contexts.

'Learning and teaching quality': our value position

We have been asked, why this particular research topic interested us. It is relevant to state here, therefore, 'where we are coming from' and the value position that led to the research and this book. We were keenly interested in the answers of pupils and teachers to questions about learning and teaching for three sets of reasons.

First, we are both products of working-class homes, 'council house' boys who, following the provision of free secondary education by way of the 1944 Education Act, were within our respective families the first to compete for secondary grammar school places, go on to higher education and become teachers. We know from long experience (whatever governments or passing politicians may say) that teaching is hard and challenging work, and that the academically well endowed child will always succeed. Our concern and commitment is for the teaching and learning of the 'many', not just the gifted few. We have enacted and believe in the validity of a *transactive* view of learning (Vygotsky 1978; Bruner 1986). We therefore see real value in knowing what the range of pupils and teachers have to say about a topic central to school effectiveness and maximum achievement for the many. In so far as we have an agenda, we would intend that the product of this research might illuminate and enhance classroom practice and achievement for all secondary school pupils.

Second, our thinking about teaching over recent years has been influenced by a particular theoretical perspective: the *quality* paradigm; that is, some of the key concepts of total quality management (TQM). The application of these have been discussed elsewhere in connection with the effectiveness of schools and the public sector generally (Murgatroyd and Morgan 1993; Morgan and Murgatroyd 1994). But of prime relevance to the quality of learning and teaching are the TQM concepts of *process* and *process owners.*

A central belief of TQM is that improvement in the quality of outcomes (in the case of schools we can translate these as significant gains in the totality of learning achievements) is obtained through improving processes. A process is defined as an activity which converts inputs into outputs. The TQM perspective believes that processes can be monitored and brought under control for improvement purposes only by gathering data from, and for use by, the people closest to that process – those who actually convert the 'inputs' into 'outputs'. In TQM terms, then, both teachers and pupils are the 'process owners' of teaching and learning, and it is only they who can significantly enhance the effectiveness of the process. Hence, the intention of our research was to obtain data from the key actors or owners of the teaching/learning process.

As teachers practising at all levels in the education system for nearly four decades, we have both been aware of the dominant curriculum ideologies pervading the British educational system, and discern a shift away from a predominantly humanitarian view of learning, through a liberal stance where education is seen as the engine of social and cultural change, to one which finds its *raison d'être* in encouraging an efficient modern economy (though we would not necessarily agree that the three are discrete in practice). So while we would recognize that recent governments have stressed economic justification for achieving 'quality' of teaching and learning in schools, this is only part of it. The competitive advantage of a highly skilled productive labour force is of course a crucial factor in a global economy and information society. But of equal, if not greater, importance is education's role in equipping each of its citizens with the character of autonomous thought and action, with the *moral sense* and civic confidence that they collectively are the ultimate government. *Quality* in education is then about character and skills, about both the architecture of the soul and the standard of living.

Our essential value position for several sets of reasons, therefore, is that we would want policy for secondary schooling in Britain to be influenced less by ideologies or political main chance seeking and more crucially by needs as expressed by the voices of the key actors in the educational arena.

Organization and scope of the chapters which follow

In this opening chapter we have set out as we see it the policy background, made clear the focus of our research, discussed the case schools where we collected the data and outlined our methods approach. Chapter 2 is about pupils' views of their learning, and is based on what the pupils said in response to core question 1. In Chapters 3 and 4 we discuss the pupils' perspectives regarding good teaching, and these are based on their answers to core questions 2, 3 and 4. Chapter 5 turns to the teachers' view of pupils' learning, and is based on the answers they gave to their core question 1. In Chapter 6 the teacher voices are on the topic of their own pedagogy, and are based on their answers to teacher core questions 2 and 3.

In Chapter 7, we compare the pupil and teacher perspectives which have so far been presented and consider the extent to which they complement or contrast with each other. In the concluding Chapter 8, we seek to draw together the research findings and discuss their implications for several categories of public policy for secondary schooling as the twenty-first century looms.

2 | Pupils and learning: why they learn more in some lessons

Among the growing number of school-based ethnographic studies over the past twenty years, there has been some reporting, albeit to a modest degree, of pupil views with regard to teacher types and the classroom practices pupils favour (for example, Woods 1979; Beynon 1985; Rudduck 1996), but we know of no reported research studies in Britain which give pupils' views of learning *per se*. How do they look on themselves as learners? When they go to the different classes in their secondary schools, do they have essentially the same learning experience, or are there significant variables of their own or others' making? What makes the difference between those lessons where they believe they learn more and those where they think they learn less? These were the kind of issues we had in mind when asking the first of our questions on learning to 207 pupil interviewees: do you think you *learn more* in some lessons than others?

Overwhelmingly (93 per cent), the pupils said that they did, and this level of response was consistent across all schools (Table 2.1), from the salubrious to the socially challenged, from the most rural to the most urban. The three pupils out of all pupil interviewees who 'didn't know' were representative of that very small minority who have turned up at various types of interview with us over the years, not really having a view on anything particular, although they were pleasant enough to talk to. We could find no common denominator to the 5 per cent of pupils who answered 'no' and who felt that they 'learned about the same' in all lessons; they were drawn from both genders and covered all ability groups.

The 193 pupils who had given an affirmative answer to our question about learning more were next asked: 'What makes *the difference* between lessons where you learn a lot and those where you don't learn much?' We wrote down their responses, which ranged from simple sentences to more elaborate answers, and analysed them for discrete statements of meaning, which we categorized. Altogether, in answers to this question, we found we could separate out 245 discrete 'reason statements', which we analysed for their essential meanings. Four main categories of reasons emerged for

Table 2.1 Learning more in some lessons than others: pupils' responses in the ten schools

Response/school	Yes	No	Don't know	Totals
A	11	0	1	12
B	33	3	0	36
C	15	3	1	19
D	18	1	1	20
E	15	1	0	16
F	17	1	0	18
G	26	2	0	28
H	19	0	0	19
I	19	0	0	19
J	20	0	0	20
Totals	193	11	3	207
Percentages	93.24	5.31	1.45	100

'learning more' in some lessons: 'something to do with the teacher'; 'something to do with me, the pupil'; 'something to do with the nature of the specific subject' being taught in the lesson; or for a 'miscellany of other reasons'. There was a very clear cut pattern to the pupils' reasons 'why they learned more', and it was one which was consistent across all schools. Substantially, they said that the main reason for learning more in some lessons than others was something to do with the teacher (Table 2.2). Their comments within this main category dealt with: teaching methods, the teacher's relations with pupils and the teacher's 'control of the class', and we shall be illustrating in detail each of these subcategories below. Across all the schools, this main category of 'something to do with the teacher' constituted a massive 60 per cent of all the separate response reasons given by pupils in answer to the question.

The second main category of responses from pupils regarding 'learning more' essentially constituted reasons that were 'something to do with me,

Table 2.2 The pupils' view of learning more in some lessons: main categories ($n = 245$)

Response category	Mean % response across all schools
Something to do with the teacher	59.8
Something to do with me, the pupil	23.3
Something to do with nature of subject	7.1
Miscellaneous reasons	9.8
Total	100

Table 2.3 Learning more in some lessons than others: main response categories – variation across the ten schools (percentage responses)

School	The teacher	The pupil	The subject	Other
A	64	18	18	0
B	51	38	6	5
C	63	21	0	16
D	54	21	0	25
E	70	25	5	0
F	64	16	4	16
G	61	24	6	9
H	64	24	4	8
I	62	14	14	10
J	45	32	14	9

the pupil'; and this accounted for almost a quarter of the responses across the ten schools, embracing replies which were essentially to do either with 'my level of interest in, or liking of the subject of the lesson' or 'my liking of the teacher taking the lesson'. We shall be examining in closer detail pupils' responses in both these and the other two main categories, but it is noteworthy that 83 per cent of all their statements focus on the two key actors in teaching and learning, the teachers and themselves. In fact, in no school, if we combine the percentages of these two main categories, do the reasons amount to less than 75 per cent (see Table 2.3). Learning more in the pupils' eyes, then, is overwhelmingly something to do with themselves or their teachers.

There is perhaps no surprise about the domination of these 'key actor' categories, but their weighting is greater than we would have anticipated. On the basis of informal staffroom conversations we have heard, it would have been reasonable to assume that factors to do with subject matters might have assumed a higher significance. In this third main category indicated in Table 2.3, that of 'something to do with the nature of the subject itself', pupil responses embraced perceptions that either there is 'more to learn in some subjects', or 'some subjects are harder than others' by their very nature.

The fourth category of miscellaneous reasons contained a wide gamut of statements: sometimes to do with school organization policy in respect of setting, streaming or mixed ability; with class size; with the length of the teaching period; with the structure of a particular course; with the fact that there is more homework in some subjects; or with the plain idiosyncratic, as we will illustrate later.

Categorization of pupil responses is remarkably similar across the schools (Table 2.3), despite variation in the number of interviewees. Clearly, as we have said, the degree to which they elaborated their responses to the question also varied. But despite these differences and those stemming from the social and demographic background of the schools, the rank order of the four categories conforms to a constant pattern. Where exceptionally this is not the case, it is a reflection of distinctive local circumstances. For example, school D has a high weighting of responses in the 'other' category, which is to be explained by the fact that this school had at the time a 'mixed ability' policy for its lower year groups, about which there was a high incidence of pupil observations in their answers to us. We now consider these four categories in detail, and we will see that there is much that the pupils tell us which bears on quality of learning and quality of teaching issues.

Something to do with the teacher

According to the pupils in all the schools, it is the teacher who is the main influence in their learning more. But what do the pupils say about the nature of this teacher influence? We found that we could further distribute the pupils' reasons into subcategories of comments which were each concerned with a particular component of teachers' work (Table 2.4).

More than half the pupils' responses are concerned with teaching methods. The remainder are broadly to do equally with interpersonal relationships with them as pupils in the learning situation, or the way teachers maintained control and order in the classroom. The ranking by pupils of these three components of a teacher's work across the ten schools (Table 2.5) is generally consistent, with one school proving to be an exception, but with teaching methods always first. The pupils' perspective regarding teachers' contribution to their learning is therefore a consistent one, whatever the social or demographic context of the particular school. Again, we can say that where the weighting of a response is higher than general, it can often be explained by the distinctive local circumstances; for example, with regard to the higher weightings given to 'control and order' in pupil responses in schools E and I. School E had asked us to undertake survey work with regard to discipline and control, as this was a concern at the time, while school I is the school we described earlier as 'socially challenged', with many problems of order endemic in local society.

Table 2.4 Why pupils learn more: the 'to do with the teacher' subcategories

Subcategory	Mean % response across all schools
To do with teaching methods	35.6
Teacher's control and order	13.95
Teacher's interpersonal relationships	10.25
Total mean % response to subcategory	59.8

Table 2.5 Why pupils learn more: variation of responses across the ten schools, 'to do with the teacher' (percentage responses)

School	Teaching methods	Teacher's control and order	Teacher's interpersonal relations
A	37	18	9
B	32	11	8
C	53	5	5
D	29	8	17
E	30	25	15
F	36	16	12
G	43	12	6
H	36	16	12
I	24	24	14
J	36	4.5	4.5

The three subcategories within the main category of 'to do with the teacher', were, of course, constructed by us from our analysis of the meanings embedded in the pupils' replies to our question, and we now need to illustrate our judgement of meanings by examples of the statements the pupils made. Assigning factors to the categories we derived from the totality of pupil responses is usually clear-cut, helped by the recurrence of certain key words. Occasionally, though, what is being said can be very close to the boundary of one subcategory or the other and could potentially be put either way, so a judgement must be made about what was the essential category of intention by the pupil. In the discussion which follows and in which we shall be citing the 'pupil voices', we indicate in parentheses, after the citation, the gender, ability and year group of the respondent making the statement. For example, (B-L-9) would mean that the statement had been made by a boy, of 'lower' ability group, in Year 9; and (G-U-7) would be referring to a girl designated by the school as upper ability from Year 7.

Teachers' methods

In response to our question about 'learning more in some lessons than others', we included in this category any statement dealing with classroom practice which was not explicitly about teacher–pupil relations or control and order in the classroom. Four aspects of teaching methods can be derived, and these came from statements by pupils of all abilities and ages and across all the schools.

There were, first, comments to do with teachers making clear what the objective of the lesson was, and about giving pupils a sense of purpose, such as:

Depends on the teacher sometimes . . . in some lessons you don't know what you are doing. (G-U-9)

Because teachers are different, some really get you down to work. (G-L-13)

Pupils frequently gave reasons for 'learning more' in some lessons which were related to whether there was suitable lesson material, whether it was presented with sufficient explanation and at an appropriate pace:

Some teachers are better than others, they go into more detail and explain; others don't explain and you are left to understand yourself . . . there are more bad ones than good. (B-M-12)

The teacher which takes you – if they don't explain it clearly and things. (G-L-11)

In some [lessons] they tell us what it is about and explain. (G-L-8)

Because some teachers have different paces; [I] learn more at faster pace. (B-M-10)

Some teachers – the way they treat you and give you extra [easier work] sheets to help you understand it a bit more. (B-L-10)

Some teachers explain more to you; others tell you to get on with it. (B-M-8)

Where the teacher explains things in the work they give us, some just hand you the sheet and say get on with it – others explain. (G-U-9)

Some don't explain well, you ask them questions and they get cross, we need to be told thoroughly more than once. (B-M-10)

If teacher shouts then you are tense – if they are calm and explain and go over things again, then you learn more. (G-M-8)

Another important focus of pupils' concern about learning more in some lessons related to the need for variety in lessons. The pupils saw *a range of activities* as a vital characteristic of effective learning. This, together with the issue of explanation, constituted by far the greatest proportion of factors they offered relating to teachers' methods:

More activities in some lessons so you achieve more. (G-M-8)

When it [the lesson] is more practical or activity based; relevant as who you like on TV for example. (M-L-10)

Try harder in some subjects because they are more interesting, e.g. tracing family history for yourself; subjects like maths, German where you play board games; don't like subjects where you do mostly writing and nothing interesting. (G-M-7)

Work where you can talk a bit, do partner work or group work. (G-M-9)

> Some lessons teachers just talk and don't give us much time to find out more – [how] to do it for ourselves. (G-U-8)

> Don't like all writing. (B-M-10)

> Not just copying out of books, where told what to do, [where they] explain what and why. I don't like total silence. (B-M-9)

> Some teachers explain more; others just tell you what to do and hope you get on with it; [also, if] you go over stuff that you have learned before, you learn a lot. (B-U-8)

> Where teacher makes it exciting – bit of fun. (B-M-8)

> Because some are more enjoyable than others. In some subjects teachers just write. It is not as interesting as when others explain. (B-M-11)

> In some lessons you enjoy learning more – some too much writing . . . boring; in languages we play games and stuff and learn more, where we get more variety. (G-U-8)

Finally, in respect of methods and 'learning more', some pupils also commented on teachers' use of visual aids:

> Some subjects use more media . . . more illustrations. (B-L-7)

> Some teachers tell us to get on with it without explaining. Best where they explain. Some use visual aids to encourage us. (B-U-8)

Pupils can therefore offer clear and insightful reasons in respect of teachers' activities as to why they think they learn more in some lessons than others. As is clear from the above citations, pupils of all ages and abilities have views on teaching methods, and these are generic across schools, for we found no case where a particular aspect of teacher activity appeared to be commented upon more in one school than in another. There is much that we could comment on here regarding the pupils' observations about teachers' methods, but we shall leave this to the next chapter, where we report the parallel and more detailed pupil views obtained on methods, when we asked a direct question about *good teaching*.

Control and order

We included in this category any statement made by pupils which conveyed meanings involving an absence of 'mucking about', the teacher being in control or the teacher creating a disciplined setting with a clear sense of work purpose to the class. To some extent, we were surprised at the emphatic way and, on occasions, the vehemence of the pupils in their comments about the desirability of control and order in the classroom for their learning more.

In some subjects there are undisciplined pupils so teacher unable to teach. (B-L-9)

There is the teacher – if the teacher can't keep control. (G-M-9)

Where there is a lot of mucking about. (G-U-10)

Where there is quietness not noise. (B-M-9)

In some classes teachers can handle individuals, others can't; also noise in the classroom. (B-M-8)

People mess around – good teacher controls us. (B-L-9)

In some lessons my friends disturb me and I can't get on with my work. (B-L-7)

Some people in your class hold you back and teachers are occupied with them because they are messing around. (G-U-8)

Some of my friends lark about and I don't learn much. (B-L-9)

Where there is mucking about – better where teacher which is strict – some allow mucking about. (B-L-10)

Where there is mucking about. (B-L-8)

You learn more if you have strict teachers. (B-L-7)

Either the teacher or who is in the class with you, people who mess around. Some teachers are not so strict and you don't work so hard. Others are stricter you really try. (B-U-10)

If the teacher has control. If children are out of control, we can't learn. (G-M-11)

Where the class is mucking about teachers don't always have strict control. (G-U-8)

In maths and English not so much messing about [because] the teacher is controlling the class. (G-L-11)

If there is a lot of noisy pupils then you don't learn much. (G-M-8)

In some lessons we are in sets; and in some lower sets, bad behaviour. (G-L-8)

A significant proportion of pupils perceive, then, the absence of 'control and order' as a major constraint on how much they learn, and the range of quotations above sharply conveys their meanings. On the one hand, they spoke of 'mucking' or 'messing' about, 'noise' and 'undisciplined' behaviour, which they find not conducive to learning. On the other hand, they point to 'keeping control', 'the need for strictness', as an absolute requirement. They are in no doubt as to where the responsibility for an ordered classroom lies.

Many pupils offer more than one reason to account for effective learning, but in the case of 'control and order', for about 10 per cent of them, it is this single factor which concerns them. This point particularly applies to those designated 'lower ability', and we established a significant relationship between the frequency of concern for control and order in 'learning more' and the lower ability group. Using chi-squared, we compared the frequency of response in respect of the three teacher factors of 'control', 'methods' and 'relationships' and the three ability groups. We found there to be a statistically significant relationship only between pupils designated 'lower ability' group and the frequency of their comments on 'control and order' in the classroom. The χ^2 measure we obtained for this comparison was 22.74, which is highly significant at the 0.001 level, and means that the likelihood of this occurring by chance is less than one in a thousand.

We think that this could be because 'low ability' pupils have experienced more classroom control and order problems as a consequence of being seated with peers who are disruptive, or just because pupils designated in this category have had lower levels of prior learning success and feel the need for more order than those more accomplished in their year group. Whatever the reason, there is clearly scope for more research on this topic, for, as the citations show, control and order in relation to learning more is a factor of concern to all ability groups. As we shall see in the next chapter, it also very much enters into a pupil's definition of a good teacher.

Teacher–pupil relations

We included in this category statements of pupils' perceptions of pupil–teacher relationships and their preferred styles. Key issues here included: 'teacher respect for pupils'; 'being socially approachable and having time for pupils'; 'being nice' and 'friendly' and 'firm'; prepared to help when the pupil was in difficulties; and, finally, speaking and communicating with pupils in an acceptable way. The following citations from all year and ability groups and both genders exemplify these points:

Where teacher respects you more ... willing to help you ... more approachable. (G-U-10)

Poor teachers shout a lot, they don't listen to pupils when they require assistance. (G-M-10)

The atmosphere – the vibes the teacher gives out – how relaxed and understanding they are if you are not sure of the work. (G-U-10)

Some teachers help you to understand more, others don't. (B-M-7)

Teachers are different – some don't have much time to help you, and some do. (G-L-8)

The teachers. Some teachers give people respect and you listen to them. (B-M-8)

Lessons you enjoy more, teachers how they speak to you and their relationships with you. (B-U-9)

I enjoy some teachers; where teachers are kind and helpful. (B-L-11)

In some lessons nobody listens, she just shouts. I asked a question and she told me to shut up; if a teacher is nice and talks to you tidy like some other teachers don't. (G-L-9)

Amount of help you get from the teacher; where you get on with the teacher. (B-M-7)

It is to do with the teachers and whether you get on with them, and the different attitudes they have to teaching. If teachers aren't strict to begin with, pupils take advantage and there is not communication. (G-U-10)

I want to learn more in some subjects in order to get a good job, in maths and English the teachers help you if you don't understand. (G-M-7)

The teacher helps more in some lessons. (B-M-10)

It depends on the teacher a lot; if they are firm but nice you learn more. In history I've made friends with the teacher and I do better now. (G-M-7)

To sum up, for effective learning the teacher manifests a helpful disposition, particularly when the work is difficult to understand; promotes nice, friendly but firm relationships; encourages personal contacts with learners; and avoids shouting.

Overall, we found that in commenting on teachers' contribution to their learning, many pupils can make the connection between methods, order and relationships. Even quite young people – as some of the comments from Year 7 pupils show – can offer perceptive and sophisticated observations on the aspects of teachers' activities which enable their learning. And while the 'lower ability' pupils might be generally less articulate, their observations are not lacking in awareness compared with the others. Interestingly, one of the more comprehensive and perceptive statements was made by a pupil of middle range ability:

One excellent teacher in history and law. I would never want to let her down. She wouldn't let you get away with not working. Her teaching methods are good, the notes provided reinforce the work, and she is very approachable and will explain; also gives regular homework work. (G-M-13)

This statement, both articulate and economical, embodies the essence of the pupils' collective views on the role of the teacher in promoting effective learning: a teacher who provides a strong learning structure with support-ive materials, has high expectations about the pupil's response and is rewarded by a positive working relationship with her learners.

Something to do with me as a pupil

It will be recalled that about a quarter of all pupils' 'learning more' rea-sons (Table 2.1) had been categorized as 'something to do with me, the pupil', and the reasons stated in this category were essentially about the pupil's attachment to the particular subject or a particular teacher. As Table 2.6 indicates, overwhelmingly the reasons given in this category are to do with interest in, liking or more rarely the pupil's performance in a subject. What comes through from the detail of the comments is their intrinsic interest in, or liking for, a subject, which causes them to work harder; and that the declaration of a 'because of the subject' reason for learning more in some lessons is by no means unconnected with the teacher. Typical comments were:

Like some subjects better than others. (B-M-8)

Because more interested in some subjects. (B-L-12)

I enjoy some subjects more than others; sometimes the way some things are taught are boring. (B-M-7)

Because I'm interested in the subject . . . e.g. in English. (B-M-12)

Because I am interested in the subject . . . interested in subjects where you can relate it to something in real life. (G-M-12)

Some teachers better at teaching. Some subjects I don't like because I'm no good at it, e.g. history – can't remember dates. (G-L-12)

I learn more where I am good at the subject, where I am not so good it is important that I am taught well. (B-L-7)

If I enjoy a subject I work harder. (B-U-7)

If you like the subject more, you listen more. (G-M-7)

Because you need some subjects you try harder than others. (B-L-8)

In the subjects I like, I concentrate more. (B-M-10)

Depends on whether you are interested in the subject. (G-M-11)

I don't listen in some I don't like it [the subject]; I don't like teachers, only some. (B-L-9)

Some lessons are more important, e.g. English, so give more attention. (G-L-8)

Table 2.6 Why pupils learn more: the 'to do with me as a pupil' subcategories

Subcategory	Mean % response across all schools
My level of interest in or liking of subject	20.35
My liking of the teacher	2.95
Total mean % response	23.3

Pupils' interest in the subject as a springboard for learning more was a significant element. The weighting of this factor, however, did vary from school to school (Table 2.7), but we are not able to account for the differences. Could the incidence of pupils 'liking the subject' reflect the quantity of good teachers in a school as defined by pupils?

Table 2.7 Why pupils learn more: variation of responses 'to do with me as a pupil' (percentage response)

School	My level of interest in, or liking of, the subject (% responses)
A	18
B	35
C	21
D	21
E	20
F	12
G	18
H	16
I	10.5
J	32

For the other subcategory to do with the pupil, only 3 per cent of reasons were concerned with 'liking the teacher' (Table 2.6), a much smaller percentage than we had expected. We believe that this incidence of 'liking the teacher' as an explanation by pupils for learning more in some lessons is substantially lower than secondary teachers and staffroom culture generally would commonly have it. Interestingly enough, this category of reason was never offered on its own, but combined with others, usually liking the subject, for example:

Liking the subject; where you are good at it; liking the teacher. (G-U-9)

Liking the teacher a lot; ones [subjects] I enjoy. (G-U-7)

If we bring together the other categories of pupil perceptions we have discussed – 'classroom practice' and 'relationships' with 'liking the teacher'

– we can hypothesize that there is more tendency to base this liking upon the teacher's technical proficiency in the core elements of his or her role rather than upon more idiosyncratic personal factors.

Something to do with nature of subject

A modest category of reasons offered by pupils (7 per cent of the total) as the explanation of where they learn more was to do with the nature of the subject itself. Examples are:

Some subjects more difficult than others. (B-U-10)

There is more to learn about in some subjects, more in science and stuff, least in PSE. (B-M-10)

Better integration of the course in [some subjects such as] chemistry. Geography is modular and more fragmented. (B-M-13)

As the citations indicate, the defining feature was that the subject was intrinsically more difficult or took a good deal more study than some others.

Other reasons

Our last category of reasons given by pupils for learning more in some lessons – less than 10 per cent of the total – includes a range of miscellaneous reasons, as the following examples indicate:

Because of more homework; because of more explanation with learning. (G-U-9)

Some teachers explain [and] give you more homework. (G-L-9)

I take more interest in a single lesson than a double one. (G-M-9)

Because there are more lessons in some subjects – also I like some subjects better than others. (B-M-8)

In some subjects you get double periods. (G-U-7)

Some teachers away a lot. (G-L-8)

Teacher absences. (B-M-11)

Setting in lessons helps doing better in those – all people who are faster learners – you can understand things better, less distraction. (B-M-9)

In sets you are not with people who are disruptive. (G-U-9)

Where I am in a mixed ability group – a real mess, people shout – setting is better. (G-M-7)

Teachers – when we have a supply teacher it's too easy, people muck around. (B-M-9)

Some lessons are taken by supply teachers and no work has been left. (B-L-9)

Class sizes – large classes take longer to get things done. (G-U-8)

Because some classes have less pupils. (B-L-9)

We had a supply teacher in physics, she did mirrors, there was lots of information – she knew a lot about it. (B-M-10)

The 'other' reasons which pupils perceived to be related to their learning more in some lesson situations were a miscellany of issues to do with: the fact that they were given more homework in some lessons; that lesson periods were of different lengths and that in some subjects there were more of them; that sometimes teachers were absent; the size of classes; whether they were in sets or mixed ability classes; and the experience of supply teachers.

The pupil perspective: what are we to make of it?

We have examined the elements that pupils generally perceived to be conducive to effective learning. We can, however, think of other factors which might have been offered, but which were hardly touched upon. For example, we were surprised that only one pupil out of more than two hundred made any reference to his or her own personal ability and the issue of learning, namely 'apart from personal ability, the teaching standard plays a large part' (G-U-9). Nor was there any reference to the employment or otherwise of study skills or work strategies which might affect their learning. Rather, in this context, they extensively associated learning with teacher delivery of lessons. Although we have commented on the degree of sophistication exercised by pupils in analysing their learning environment, we see the absence of reference to what they themselves bring as indicative of the fact that they have little developed sense of ownership in the teaching–learning process. In short, they portray themselves for the most part in a recipient rather than a partnership role with their teachers.

Regarding the dogs which did bark, however, the pupil perspective of priorities in 'learning more' is very clear (Table 2.8). We constructed eight subcategories of reasons embedded in the answers the pupils gave to our question, and when these are displayed in rank order it is easy to see how extensively teacher-related factors dominated. If we define 'good learning' as situations where pupils learn a lot rather than a little, more rather than less, then the pupils' perspective, irrespective of how they are categorized – by gender, by ability or by year group – is unequivocally clear. 'Good

Table 2.8 Why pupils learn more in some subjects than others: summary ranking by category

Category	% mean	Rank
To do with teaching methods	35.6	1
Pupil's liking or level of interest in the subject	20.35	2
Teacher's classroom control and order	13.95	3
Teacher's relationships with pupils	10.25	4
Miscellaneous	9.8	5
Some subjects are harder than others	5.0	6
Pupil's liking of teacher	2.95	7
More to learn in some subjects	2.1	8
Eight construct categories of reason	100	

learning', as expressed in their responses, is overwhelmingly down to the work of teachers, in teachers' work resolved into the three principal components: presentation of lessons; maintenance of good order in the classroom; and the promotion of appropriate social relationships.

This chapter has been concerned with analysis of pupil perceptions about their own learning, although, as we have seen, the principal thrust of their comments has been directed to the role of the teacher. In the next chapter we shall be considering their responses to a question more directly concerned with teaching, and, as we shall show, much more detail about this crucial element emerges.

In Table 2.8 the only other category of explanation which carries any real weight in response to the question about learning more, 20 per cent of the totality of pupils' explanation, was that of 'their level of interest or liking of the subject'. The quality of teaching and the level of interest in the subject being taught are, then, the prime factors for good learning in the view of the pupil. We do not really know why pupils find more interest in some subjects than in others, and, given the constraints of limited time with them, we were not able to follow this up by further questioning. We can reasonably assume that there may always be a preferential orientation towards a particular subject area by the individual.

What we are unsure about, though, is the interaction effect between very good teaching and the degree of liking towards a particular subject. We judge from what we have heard pupils say, in these and other schools, that even where pupils may not have a ready or natural interest in a particular subject, it can be ignited and developed by teacher actions. We say this because in our interviews we have found situations where all our interviewees across certain year groups expressed great interest in, and satisfaction with, the lesson experiences in a particular subject by a particular teacher. The most emphatic examples we noted were to do with the teaching of drama, technology, science and maths to certain year groups in different schools. What the pupils had said to us clearly linked their interest and enthusiasm to how the teacher related to them and presented the subjects. Yet these were all subjects for which a wide range of interest levels had been expressed in the other schools. Are we to conclude then, that, while there will always be differing presenting levels of pupil interest for particular subjects, there are some teachers who can make all pupils interested in their subject? More important still, do these qualities inhere in the general characteristics of the teacher as a person or can they be skills learned by trainees and developed as they gather professional experience?

The message from pupils in this chapter is that 'good learning' over-whelmingly derives from the actions of teachers and only in a subordinate way to pupils' attachment to the particular subject. They do not connect the quality of their learning with their own abilities, the effort they put in or particular study techniques on their part.

3 | Pupils and teachers: why some teachers are better than others

In preceding chapters we set out our analysis of pupils' replies to the question about their own learning. We showed that these responses focused mainly upon the teachers' role as a major force in affecting the rate at which they learned, with factors to do with themselves and the subject they were following taking subordinate positions. We also argued that pupils were capable of stating their views on pedagogy in a relatively sophisticated way, and contrasted this with the general tendency to omit any systematic exploration of their perceptions by education policy makers at all levels.

When we had interviewed pupils in connection with TVEI innovations in schools in the 1980s, we sometimes received within the broader context of their answers, views about 'good' and 'bad' teachers, even though we had not asked for them. We resolved that, when the opportunity arose, we would try systematically to find out more about this topic. So within the context of our 'quality of learning' project interviews, we asked, as we indicated in Chapter 1, the following question: *Do you think that some of your teachers are better as teachers than others?* If they answered in the affirmative, we followed up with: *what then makes some teachers better than others – what makes the difference between those who are good and those who are not so good?* This chapter presents and discusses the answers we received from pupils to this area of enquiry.

As Table 3.1 shows, the clear majority of pupils across all schools thought that some teachers teach better than others. Even among the 12 per cent who answered 'no' to this question, up to about a half subsequently made some qualifying remarks which implied that, while they thought all their teachers were good, some teachers' methods were different from, and sometimes preferred over, others. For example:

No, they are all just as good but they have different ways of teaching – some ways are more enjoyable, more activity in the lessons – more variety. (G-U-8)

Table 3.1 'Some teachers are better than others': pupils' responses in the ten schools

School	Yes	No	Don't know	Total
A	7	4	1	12
B	33	3	0	36
C	15	3	1	19
D	20	0	0	20
E	13	3	0	16
F	16	2	0	18
G	24	4	0	28
H	17	2	0	19
I	19	0	0	19
J	16	4	0	20
Total	180	25	2	207
%	(87)	(12)	(1)	(100)

No, all good; all kind and generous – they explain before you do the work [but] some are stricter. (B-L-7)

No, all about the same – but if teacher not doing own specialist subject, not so good; better teachers get pupils involved. (G-U-7)

The 180 pupils who replied in the affirmative to this question gave (as with our earlier question about the extent of their learning) replies which ranged from simple sentences to more elaborate statements of opinion, all of which we again analysed for the discrete statements of meaning within them, and which we categorized. Altogether, we found that, from these 180 pupils, we could separate out 268 discrete 'reason statements' to explain why they thought some teachers taught better than others. We found that all these statements could be attributed to one or other of three main categories of response, which we have called 'classroom practices', 'teacher relationships' or 'other' (Table 3.2).

The first two of these categories cover over 90 per cent of the pupils' 268 statements. The category of 'classroom practices' covers all those statements made by pupils which are essentially to do with the technical or *task* qualities of teaching rather than the *person* aspects of the role, such as: methods of presentation and types of learning activities in lessons; the giving of explanation and feedback; and control and order in the classroom. In contrast, the second main category, which we have called 'teacher relationships', is essentially embracing *affective* qualities and all those skills which are *person-oriented*, such as: how the teacher communicates to pupils; the nature of her or his interpersonal social relations or style; and the posture of encouragement or expectation of pupils which he or she displays.

We are not suggesting that the two main categories are totally clear-cut. Given the nature of teaching in which the *person* and *task* skills required can be so interwoven, there will inevitably be marginal statements that could reasonably be attributed to the affective or the task category. For example, and to take the aspect of 'humour', pupils sometimes referred to the capacity for humour as an attribute of a teacher's interpersonal relationships, while on other occasions the reference to humour was connected with classroom task activity. We let context rule the categorizing. The small 'other' or miscellaneous category covers those meanings in pupils' statements which were not directed at teachers' generic person or task role aspects, but at specific attributes to do with a teacher's subject, or the type of teacher, in terms of whether they were permanent or supply etc.

Table 3.2 'Some teachers teach better – why?':
main categories of response ($n = 268$)

Main category	Mean % across all schools
To do with classroom practices	59
To do with teacher relationships	37
To do with other factors	4
Total	100

As Table 3.2 indicates, the explanation for better teaching in the perception of pupils is mostly to do with the task behaviours of teachers in the classroom, although the difference in the weight of comments given to this category from that of teacher relationships is not great. In fact, in general terms from this broad picture, it can be concluded that good teaching in the eyes of pupils exhibits a balance between the 'person' and 'task' skills, with other constituents of good teaching or hallmarks of good teachers counting for a small minority of 'other' factors.

The variation of response across schools, in the main, conformed to this same rank order of importance: in all but two schools, the number of 'task' or classroom practice reasons which pupils gave were greater than those for teacher relations (see Table 3.3). In schools A and J this rank order was reversed, and there we received the largest proportions of pupils' responses rating the factor of 'teacher–pupil relations' of first rank importance in good teaching. This may indicate in schools A and J a generally higher than average satisfaction with the teachers, or it might arise from the processes of sampling. What does seem clear to us, though, is that there is no relationship between the weighting of these categories of response and the social context of the ten schools. If, for example, we examine the data from schools E and I, the most affluent and the most deprived of the schools among our ten, the response patterns are very similar. The pupils in both these schools gave the highest (and same percentage

Table 3.3 'Some teachers teach better – why?': variation across schools in main categories of response (percentage responses)

School	Classroom practices	Teacher–pupil relations	Other
A	36	55	9
B	63	35	2
C	53	47	0
D	54	42	4
E	72	14	14
F	53	43	4
G	67	33	0
H	63	29	8
I	72	25	3
J	36	52	12
Means	56.9	37.5	5.6

of) comments, in answers to our question about what makes some teachers better than others, to classroom practice factors.

The careful reader will have noted that the 'means' displayed in Table 3.3 are different from those in Table 3.2, and this difference is to be explained by the sort of variations which derive from 'rounding' to whole percentages in standardizing for group size. Because Table 3.3 is essentially displaying individual schools or subcategories of the macro group, 'all schools' (of Table 3.2), the desire to produce simple straightforward tables by 'roundings' has produced slightly different outcomes for the same data. For example, and with regard to the category of 'other reasons' which pupils gave to explain why some teachers are better than others, there were twelve actual pupil statements included in this category, which is 4.47 per cent of all pupils' reasons, which we rounded down to 4 per cent because it was nearer that than 5 per cent. In Table 3.3, however, the mean percentage in the 'other' category is the product of the 'roundings' of percentages from the small prime numbers involved for individual schools, and this produced a mean of 5.6 rather than 4.47. We therefore need to be very cautious when quantification is applied to qualitative data such as these, particularly when numbers are small, lest we fall into the trap of seeing the figures produced as strictly accurate measures, which they are not. They are, however, indicative evidence of the weightings, consistency and representativeness of perspectives on a particular topic by a particular group, which speak for themselves, instead of our merely asserting perspectives based on the overall impression we gained by observation. For this reason, we are committed to displaying data in tabular form alongside giving citations of what the participants said to us.

As we said earlier, it is not the numerical aspects of what the pupils had to say that are important to issues of quality in teaching and learning, but the nature and range of meanings in their statements, and the perceptiveness of their comments that we take to be of greater significance. We now consider in turn each of the main categories of pupil response regarding 'good teaching' and look in some detail at what they said to us.

Table 3.4 'Some teachers teach better – why?': good classroom practices (all schools, $n = 157$)

Subcategory	Mean % response
To do with methods of presentation and learning activities	22.8
To do with explanation or giving of feedback	23.2
To do with classroom control and order	10.9
Total mean % response to subcategory	56.9

'Classroom practices' and good teaching

As we showed above, alongside 'teacher–pupil relations', the other substantial category of factors which pupils express as a constituent of 'good teaching' is that which we labelled 'classroom practices'. In this set of meanings, we included those statements which were essentially referring to the *task* rather than the *person* aspects of the difference between 'good' and 'less good' teaching voiced by the pupils. These 'task' or 'classroom practice' statements accounted for nearly 60 per cent of all the reasons pupils gave in differentiating good teaching (Table 3.2), and within them there were three clear subcategories of comment to do with presentation, explanation and order in the classroom context (Table 3.4). We discuss each of these in turn.

Methods of presentation and learning activities

Within their criteria for good teaching, pupils spell out very clearly the general principles they find most acceptable. A teacher's presentation must first of all be interesting and exciting:

How they present the work to you so not tedious and boring. (B-U-9)

Good teachers . . . make the work interesting. (B-M-9)

Poor teacher is not able to generate interest in the topic. (B-M-7)

They need to make the subject interesting and vary the teaching lessons. (G-M-12)

Some make subject more exciting. (G-M-10)

Some make lessons more interesting; teaches [*sic*] it in a way that is interesting – then we get involved. (B-U-10)

A significant component of an interesting lesson for pupils is variety of approach. One in which writing or teacher talk predominates as a single activity is not acceptable:

Some have got different ways of teaching – best way to do it is to have a mix of methods. (G-M-8)

Teachers who do it all by talking . . . class gets bored and order goes. (G-M-9)

If they talk all lesson dictating notes not good; good teacher gives you a chance to discuss. (B-M-10)

The way they talk to you; some make it fun – make it interesting. Bad teachers are those who just write on board and say get on with it. (B-M-8)

Some make things exciting, rather than just someone who talks and we just write. They [the lessons] are more well teached [*sic*] than the others. (G-M-7)

Some talk for the whole lesson. (G-U-11)

Some teachers get to be boring. If they just dictate or read out of a book, you get distracted. (G-M-11)

Some go on all lesson [with] write on board and copy it; others tell us and help us. (B-M-9)

Teachers who try different ways of teaching. Some teachers just make you copy things from a book or the board; there is need for variety and encouraging us to ask questions. (G-U-10)

Pupils also link these general principles of presentation with the need for them to be active, ideally having the opportunity to take part in a range of activities:

Some teachers make lessons more interesting with activities such as those in English. (G-U-9)

Where teacher makes it exciting, e.g. when teacher dramatize (English teacher always helps) [whereas] geography teacher makes us copy out paragraphs. (B-M-8)

Making things concrete in everyday terms and giving examples. (G-U-11)

Some teachers just talk and expect us to take it all down; others give more activities and practical work which gives us a better understanding of it ourselves. (B-M-9)

Making lessons more interesting – teachers who try different ways of teaching. Some teachers just make you copy things from a book or the board; there is need for variety and encouraging us to ask questions. (G-U-10)

The best teachers give us work and show us how to do it. (G-L-10)

In relating activities to good teaching, pupils clearly want *active learning*, with more responsibility for their own learning and less expository teaching tightly under teacher control. In particular, we noted in these statements the approval of 'having a chance to discuss', 'encouraging us to ask questions' and 'getting involved' as general indicators of the importance of active learning to pupils. In making responses like this, of course, pupils continue to place their teachers at the centre of the learning process, but are pointing up the importance of the interplay between the two roles. Active learning has been defined as:

> any activities where pupils are given a marked degree of autonomy and control over the organisation, conduct, and direction of the learning activity. Most usually such activities involve problem-solving and investigational work and may be individualised . . . or involve small-group collaboration (such as small group discussion, a role playing simulation or a collaborative project). In essence, active learning may usefully be contrasted with expository teaching which is tightly under the teacher's control . . . active learning can sometimes offer a much more powerful experience or insight into what is to be learnt than expository teaching.
>
> (Kyriacou 1991: 42)

In their own way, and in their own language, the pupils we surveyed reflect these issues, showing approval of instances where active learning opportunities are offered to them. They are asking to be given *more* to do, more variation, more occupation, more *team* stuff and more entertaining tasks. All of these at their best are equally as much under a teacher's tight control as are traditional didactic methods, but self-evidently such devolved activity methods are very much more demanding of a teacher's preparation time and involvement in the classroom.

Pupils perceive that interesting and exciting material with relevant activities also needs to be at an appropriate level and pace:

You work at your own pace. (B-M-7)

Give you right amount and level of work; strict; don't give you work without explanation. (B-G-7)

Good teaching makes you work then gives you a rest; poor teachers make you write all the time. (G-M-7)

Pupils are essentially reflecting here the good teaching precept of matching work to pupils which takes account of their interests and needs at a level where they can achieve and make optimum progress.

Explaining or giving feedback

Approaching 40 per cent of the ways that pupils differentiate between their teachers concern judgements on a teacher's ability to explain. As Table 3.4 indicates, they put those teacher actions we have included under the umbrella of *presentation* and the whole aspect of *explanation and feedback* at virtually the same level. In the following citations, pupils are emphatically pointing up the need for teachers to explain:

Some just give you work. [They] don't go through it and explain. Where they are prepared to go over it again . . . to explain it fully again. (B-M-10)

Explanation . . . very important they go into the detail of the explanation and be greeted properly. (B-U-12)

[Where they] make sure you understand – spend a lot of time explaining it – open to questions and don't mind going back over things. Where they teach with examples so that you solidify. (G-U-11)

Better ones explain subject thoroughly; they help you a lot so you definitely know what you have to do. (B-M-10)

The way they explain things – you can understand more with some than with others. Some teachers are vague – others get to the point of what needs to be done. (G-M-10)

Some teachers will explain it again if you don't understand and then if you still don't understand they will explain it again in a different way, [but] some get uptight if you ask them – uptight, they get snappy, a bit ratty. (B-U-7)

A good teacher explains, then goes through examples. (B-M-12)

How they explain work. (G-M-9)

Some teachers rush through and don't explain it properly. (G-U-10)

Where they don't give you work without explanation. (B-M-7)

Some teachers explain things more. They explain everything you have to do like. Others don't. (G-L-9)

Some teachers not bothered if you ask questions of them; good teachers explain what to do if you are stuck and will explain it over and over again. (G-M-10)

Pupils also associate 'good' teaching with explanation which is made not just to the whole class, but also individually. This seems to be a need expressed more often by lower ability group pupils than others:

> Best is where you get activities or where teachers come to you personally to explain it to you. (B-L-8)

> Good teachers help you learn in a better way instead of saying do this or that. [They] explain, helping, and showing us how to do it. (B-M-9)

> Some have different ways of teaching than others; a good teacher makes us understand more. If you do a topic, he keeps on until we have the hang of it; they help you a lot. They sit down with me – I'm deaf in one ear, and ask if I've understood. (G-L-8)

> They come over and help you more; they do a lot of writing and explain it. But in maths do a lot of writing on blackboard but don't explain it much. (B-M-9)

> Some teachers explain things; others make you copy from the board; they talk to you and try to make things simpler. If you don't understand things [in maths] the teacher comes over and makes it easier; he breaks the sums down into parts. Shows you examples. (B-L-9)

In linking *explanation* to 'good' teaching, pupils particularly deprecate the instruction of 'just get on with it'. This was the phrase we were to hear most frequently throughout our conversations with pupils on this topic. As the responses which follow show, for pupils there is a lack of *willingness* to explain implied here:

> Good teachers explain carefully; some explain nicely. Some put a sheet of paper in front of you and say 'get on with it'. (B-L-8)

> Some explain in more detail; others say just get on with it. (B-L-10)

> Where they don't explain but say 'get on with it'; You bring it to the teacher to ask about something and they say you haven't been listening. There is a difference between listening and understanding. (G-M-9)

> Good teacher explains more; bad teacher just gives you a work sheet and tells you to get on with it. (G-M-7)

Simply writing up material on the blackboard so that pupils can work from it does not, of course, imply that they are clear about their task. It should be supplemented, pupils think, by oral explanation:

> Some don't explain what they have written on the blackboard. (G-L-7)

> Teachers who explain and speak more clearly; some teachers have scruffy writing on the board. (B-M-10)

If they explain and you don't understand and they come and help you a bit further; they not only talk but write on the board with diagrams. (B-M-8)

As we have found for all other components of teacher activity, the use of humour coupled with explanation is rated highly:

Someone who can explain in depth but can have fun. (B-M-8)

Some explain things better than others; you can have a bit of a laugh with them. (B-M-10)

We also received some perceptive statements to do with what we see to be the 'cousins' of explanation, namely reinforcement and feedback. Feedback is not only of practical use to pupils in identifying problems or indicating succesful work, but also conveys that progress is being monitored. Examples of statements connecting 'feedback' with good teaching we received include:

Some go back on things and help you a lot; others do it just the once. (G-M-10)

A good teacher uses homework and review of previous work to check understanding, poor teaching doesn't know where you are, there is no feedback or review of previous work. (G-U-9)

This last statement really underlines how much pupils value human interaction, and implies that a poor teacher doesn't know where 'I am' and doesn't care.

Two issues immediately arise from the pupils' remarks. There is the perceived lack of a willingness to explain sufficiently on the part of some teachers, and more generally that of the effectiveness of the explanation when it is given. If we make the assumption that all teachers believe that they are explaining sufficiently and effectively what they are presenting to their pupils, what are we to make of the mismatch demonstrated between such intention and the reality revealed by a significant segment of pupil perceptions? Does the astonishing weight that pupils give to good *explaining* in their views on good teaching arise for the following reasons?

First, because of endemic differences in learning style which exist among pupils, teachers' explanations work for some pupils but not for others; second, some teachers are just giving insufficient explanation. We would venture that the root cause of what pupils have highlighted is that some teachers are introducing a topic and assuming that the required response by their pupils can be made in one leap – so that there are steps missing between the stages, between the teacher laying out the ground and then requiring a response from pupils. Consequently, they are not using a sufficient range of explanatory techniques or activities at the whole class, nor at the individual level.

According to Brown and Armstrong (cited in Kyriacou 1991: 36), there are five basic skills to effective explaining:

clarity and fluency: through defining new terms clearly and appropriate use of explicit language; *emphasis and interest*: making good use of voice, gestures and appropriate use of explicit language; *using examples*: appropriate in type and quality; *organisation*: presence of a logical sequence and use of link words and phrases; *feedback*: offering a chance for pupils to ask questions and assessing learning outcomes.

There is also some significant research which has demonstrated empirically that teachers who are better explainers do bring about more effective learning (e.g. Roehler and Duffy 1986). What such research has shown is that different students interpret instructional explanations differently, so that explanations must include a guided set of progressive opportunities for students to develop conceptual awareness of how to use the skill or knowledge being learned and be given the opportunity to verbalize and express different opinions about how to do the tasks set. Rather than 'dumping it' on to the student, teachers must therefore focus on gradually devolving the responsibility for doing the skill from themselves to the student, the very antithesis of 'just get on with it'. It seems to us that the sheer weight and importance that pupils give to *explanation* in their definitions of 'good' teaching calls out for more open discussion as a part of pedagogy in general, but this is a topic we shall take up again when we consider the implications for policy of the research findings as a whole.

Classroom control and order

In Chapter 2, we saw that pupils believe that a teacher's classroom 'control and order' enables them (the pupils) to learn more. It was therefore no surprise when we received this same category of comments within the range of answers to our question about what makes the difference between good and bad teaching. Statements by pupils drawn from the whole range (ability, gender, year group) make their position clear: they want control and order in their classrooms, and those teachers considered defective in this area are regarded as bad teachers.

Some more strict, more experience know how to control a class, some don't. (G-U-8)

Some teachers . . . allow distractions and disruptions. (G-M-11)

It is no good if there is no class discipline. (B-L-12)

Should be more discipline in the class with some teachers. (B-M-9)

Good teacher disciplines people more; more order. (G-U-8)

The control they have on the people in the class. (G-M-10)

Some let you get away with a lot so pupils just mess around. (G-L-12)

If they can't control a class they are not good teachers. (B-L-11)

Good teachers can keep control, bad teachers can't keep control and can't have a laugh. (B-U-12)

Moreover, the implication of many pupil comments was for teachers to be more strict. Our finding, as was the case for Rudduck (1996), was that pupils favoured *strict* teachers. Indeed, Rudduck found that even the ring-leaders of disruption in the classroom felt, after leaving school, that their achievement would have been greater had their teachers been more strict. This raises some pertinent questions about training for being 'strict', for keeping control and order in secondary classrooms.

It is important to stress, however, that our interviewees were not defining strict in a cheerless, stern or arid sense, but as the need for a balance of firm order and purpose with social acceptability. They are seeking security and safety in their learning environment, but the importance to pupils of a degree of humour and 'having fun' (Woods 1979) comes into their definition of good teaching:

And how strict they are; if some pupils mess about, half the lesson is spent in controlling. (B-U-10)

Stricter teachers get you to listen more carefully; some teachers can't control the class [so] you can't get to listen. (B-M-10)

And with strict teachers you get on with your work. (G-M-10)

Strictish but not soft – not afraid of class, strict enough to make us learn, have a laugh. (G-U-9)

Control – too much discipline and stuff can put you off – makes you feel insecure; or not too slack on the other hand, a happy medium, where you can have a laugh and a joke but not too far. (G-U-10)

Keeping order; making lessons fun and not 'that's your work get on with it'. (G-M-9)

Why do some teachers have success with order and control and others fail? There seems to be a dearth of research findings offering answers to this question, apart from those of Kounin (1970), who categorized the teacher skills associated with orderly classrooms with idiosyncratic terms such as 'withitness' and 'thrusts and dangles'. 'Withitness' consisted in giving the pupils the impression that the teacher had 'eyes in the back of her head', the facility to scan the class frequently and make regular timely and accurate remarks to show that she is missing nothing, even when she does not intervene in inattentive behaviour. 'Thrusts and dangles' Kounin saw as contributing to classroom disorder: 'teachers should not interrupt pupil work precipitously and neither should they leave issues incomplete and unresolved.' We think this whole area goes well beyond such factors as these, and is one still to be fully explored by systematic research.

Having presented and discussed the three subcategories of 'classroom practices' as if they were discrete reasons for differentiating between 'good' and 'less good' teaching, we should emphasize that pupils were well able to link these categories together in their views of good teaching:

> Good teachers can keep control, give you respect and know their subject . . . bad teachers can't keep control and can't have a laugh. (B-U-12)

> Explanations make the difference, down to earth, friendly, better attitudes towards pupils . . . commitment to ensure that pupils learn. (G-U-13)

> Where there is a friendly atmosphere, not an aggressive teacher; where explains things carefully and helps. (B-U-8)

> Good teachers explain and help you. (B-L-7)

> Help you a lot; give you right amount and level of work; strict; don't give you work without explanation. (B-M-7)

> Ones who don't shout, but who talk through the work with you and explain how to do it. (G-M-9)

> Control; explain better and have more patience, not 'I've told you once now get on with it'; gets on with pupils. (B-L-10)

We have already implied that we think pupils show a good degree of sophistication in their perceptions of the classroom practices we discussed earlier, and we think this is very true with regard to their comments on control and order; they are aware of the costs of the teacher failing to control disorder problems: 'there is less time for teaching me'. What the pupils want is a happy medium in a well ordered classroom with the teacher capable of exercising control, tempered with a lightness and humour that does not make the learning environment seem oppressive. In this respect, our findings corroborate those by Nash (1973), Gannaway (1976) and Rudduck (1996), which have shown that good teachers succeed in reconciling the opposites of freedom and control by adopting a middle course, by generating freedom within order, whereas those whom pupils see to be poor teachers either sanction excessive freedom or are inflexible.

Teacher–pupil relations and 'good teaching'

We have noted that nearly 40 per cent of reasons for some teachers being seen as better than others (Table 3.2) can be categorized under the heading of 'teacher–pupil relations'. Within this category, three different types of comment can be inferred: to do with the nature of teachers' interpersonal attitudes or postures; about the way that teachers spoke to, or communicated with, pupils; and the way that teachers demonstrated their commitment to their pupils' learning by their stated expectations or the

Table 3.5 'Some teachers teach better – why?': good teacher–pupil
'relationships' (*n* = 99)

Subcategory	Mean % response
Teacher's interpersonal style or posture	28.6
The way they communicate	6.3
Their expectations, commitment and encouragement	2.6
Total mean % response to subcategory	37.5

ways in which they encouraged them. The relative weightings of each of
these three subcategories derived from pupils' comments about teacher–
pupil relationships and good teaching are shown in Table 3.5. We have,
therefore three clear subcategories or constructs within the teacher–pupil
relationship component of 'good' and 'less good' teaching.

Clearly, the essence of the perspective is that, from the pupils' viewpoint, *good teaching* has a great deal to do with how teachers treat them
and speak to them. Pupils of both genders and all ages and abilities emphasize first that good teachers are helpful, approachable, kind and nice,
but the really key word to describe the relationship they perceive in a
good teacher is *helpful*:

Some are angry and some are kind. (G-L-7)

A good teacher is able to help pupils. (B-L-9)

A good teacher helps you a lot – not too much homework. (B-L-9)

How they treat you if you ask for help ... that they don't say 'why
didn't you listen first time?' (G-U-10)

If they are helpful and encourage you when you have a problem;
when they don't shout and are understanding. (G-M-11)

Some teachers are more helpful; explain more. (G-L-11)

A good teacher is a helpful teacher ... explains a lot. (B-M-12)

Teachers have to care; some don't seem to care. (G-M-12)

Pupils also indicate that a corollary of the helpful, caring attitude with
good teachers is approachability both ways: that they will come to help
you, and that you are more prepared to go to them. The value being expressed is closeness and physical proximity versus distance and remoteness:

They come over and help you more. (B-M-9)

Also, if they help you, if they are approachable, you will go to them
for help. (G-U-10)

They come over and help you more; they do a lot of writing and explain it. In maths do a lot of writing on blackboard but don't explain it much. (B-M-9)

Allied with the posture of helpfulness and approachability, another interpersonal hallmark of good teachers was that they maintain friendly, happy social relationships with them, in which there is mutual respect, some humour and fun:

Where they are polite to pupils – helpful – help us to get better. (B-M-7)

The best teachers treat us as young adults. (G-U-7)

If teachers make friends with you, you will do it. If they just say 'do this', 'do that' it makes you not sure. (G-M-7)

Some more friendly, have a laugh, listen more – they help more. (B-M-8)

[Good teachers] try to make friends, have a laugh now and then; bad teachers look down on you. (B-M-9)

A good relationship with the teacher gets you on the same wavelength. (G-U-9)

Whether they get on with the class or not – can create a relaxed atmosphere. (G-U-9)

Not like friends but have respect personally, [can be] both funny and serious. (B-M-9)

If teachers are friendly and kind, we'll do more for them. Some teachers are strict and you'll work for them. But you still work more for friendly teachers; if teachers are fair and explain what you have done wrong. (G-M-9)

Good teachers give more freedom. (B-M-9)

Respect both ways – if you respect the teacher and the teacher respects you. (G-U-10)

[Best] listen more to us. I just get on with them. (B-L-10)

Some have a better relationship; teachers which are down to earth . . . on a level with you. (G-U-11)

Where we get on with the teacher and they give help. (G-M-11)

Good pupil relations with the teacher, getting through to pupils by making friends. (G-U-12)

While a positive disposition towards interpersonal relationships on the part of the teacher is the main constituent of this category, communication is also an element important to pupils. In particular, they react strongly against teachers who shout at them. In fact, 'shout' is the key word in pupils' statements in this context. When we have been in schools in the past talking with a teacher or a pupil in a room on our own, we have sometimes been jolted by the noise of a teacher shouting very loudly at a pupil. Our data confirm that this is an aspect of teachers' communication with pupils on which there is a clear and unequivocal pespective. Pupils universally associate shouting with bad teachers.

Some shout when you have done nothing wrong – really bossy. (B-L-8)

[Not good] if they shout a lot. (G-M-7)

A poor teacher shouts a lot. (G-U-7)

I don't like shouting for no reason. (B-U-7)

Sometimes teachers get in a mood and shout, but a good teacher has a great deal of patience with pupils and does not shout. (G-U-8)

'Some teachers can't control so we don't learn anything. Some scream and shout but pupils don't listen to them. (G-U-9)

[Those] that don't shout as much. (B-L-11)

Some teachers are better than others because they don't shout so much, not bad tempered. (G-M-10)

[Good teachers] don't shout and are understanding. (G-M-11)

You can't talk to [some of] them without them snapping your head off – but will tell you if you are not getting on with your work. (B-U-12)

Ones who don't shout but who talk through the work with you. (G-M-9)

[Some teachers are better than others] because they don't shout so much . . . not bad tempered; [where] you can speak confidentially to some and they won't tell others. (G-M-10)

Some shout; some are nice. (G-L-8)

With regard to communication (and all other aspects of teacher behaviour for that matter), the teachers who are are always appreciated by pupils:

- have time for pupils – 'Some are too busy, they have their own work to do and say "don't bother me too much – get on with it"' (G-L-8);
- can use humour – 'A good teacher is humorous, not too strict, doesn't tell you to be quiet all the time' (B-M-8);
- will talk personally and confidentially with pupils – 'You can speak confidentially to some, they won't tell others (G-M-10);

We can observe in pupils' comments a linking of 'how the teacher communicates' with a high priority placed by them upon an orderly and disciplined class atmosphere. In part, it can be readily appreciated that the shouting of a teacher represents the latter's own frustration with the unruliness as well as apparent inattention on the part of some individual learners. The essential point here is that their rejection of the teachers' need to shout is a reinforcement of the pupils' preference for a calm and ordered working atmosphere.

The final constituent which emerges in this section concerns the extent to which teachers invite commitment and confidence from pupils or set expectations and encourage them. The key words used by pupils here are *make, push* or *press*. Pupils recognize these aspects of the total mix of skills and abilities needed to make a good teacher:

Best teachers make you work hard. (B-L-7)

Make you believe in yourself. (G-L-9)

Poor teaching is too strict, does not encourage and give credit. (B-U-10)

And if they push you its better. (G-U-10)

Teachers who interest and then press me. (B-L-11)

Good teachers know your ability; they can push you to your limit. (G-M-11)

When they recognize your difficulties – sort things out when they get out of hand. (B-L-10)

Better attitudes towards pupils, commitment to ensure that pupils learn. (G-U-13)

As we indicated above, pupil comments can connect the use of humour with all aspects of 'good' and 'not so good' teaching, and they indicate that its role and boundaries in class atmosphere need to be defined:

Some put humour into things; some are grumpy all the time; some have fun and make you learn. (B-M-9)

Have a sense of humour so they can take some stick [in conversation]. (B-U-8)

Teacher who likes a bit of fun – not too strict. (G-M-11)

Teachers who can have a bit of fun; not too easy going and not too hard. (B-M-7)

Some teachers don't have a laugh and a joke; some make lessons interesting. (B-L-9)

Pupils therefore voice many comments on a range of aspects connecting good teaching with teacher–pupil relationships. We concur with Gardner (1983) and Rudduck (1996) that pupils place tremendous emphasis on the need for good interpersonal relationships with understanding teachers who are prepared to listen; and that pupils perceive that learning takes place best where there is a mutually shared understanding between teachers and pupils, the product of what Woods (1996) has termed 'negotiative discussion'. Pye (1988, cited in Kyriacou 1991: 166), in his analysis of skilful teaching, used the phrase 'solicitous tenderness' to describe the mixture of warmth, reassurance, kindness and tact shown by skilful teachers in their interactions with pupils. The pupils we spoke with, of all abilities and ages across the ten comprehensive schools, would agree with this.

Pye also notes a study by Grace (1984) which draws attention to the fact that a high proportion of outstanding teachers in inner-city comprehensive schools were skilful in developing good rapport with potentially difficult and demanding adolescents. He concluded that skilful teachers were able to convey a personal manner in interaction with an individual pupil during a private exchange in which the mutual respect and rapport established was particularly evident. This Pye categorized as a situation in which the teacher and pupil were 'acknowledging' each other, where they had established a personal relationship which was separate from, yet still part of, the relationship that the teacher had with the class as a whole. Again, our findings are wholly congruent with this view.

In Chapter 2, we showed that pupils believe the quality of their relationships with their teachers to be an important reason why they learn more. Here, we have shown that pupils also in significant part define 'good teachers' and 'good teaching' according to teachers' interpersonal behaviour. Pupils are emphatic: they want teachers as persons who create a relationship with them, rather than what have, by contrast, been called *teacher bureaucrats* (Woods 1979).

Good teachers – the 'other' factors

It will be recalled (Table 3.2) that in addition to 'teacher–pupil relations' and 'classroom practices', there were some 'other' reasons given by pupils to differentiate good teaching, and this 5 per cent of the total embraced the issue of supply teachers, the length of a teacher's experience and the connection between the teacher and the subject.

Supply teachers were almost always compared unfavourably with the pupils' regular teachers:

> Lots of teachers go on courses and we get supply teachers who are 'lost' and we get confused . . . all we do is given something to read, we don't learn anything. (B-M-7)

> Some can't handle children – normal teachers better than supply. (G-L-8)

Sometimes, but not always, pupils connected better teaching with the length of a teacher's experience:

> Length of experience – they know what you are like; you know what they are like. (G-L-10)

> Experience. (B-M-10)

> If teacher is new they are not used to teaching. (G-U-7)

> Some been teaching longer. Some help the pupils a lot, explain it easier/more. (B-M-9)

> Where they like working with children – younger teachers make lessons interesting. (B-L-8)

Pupils do not have much to say about the subject expertise of teachers and, as we shall show later, neither do the teachers themselves give it any emphasis within their views of good teaching and learning. Only 2 per cent of all comments focused on this issue, despite the fact that, for teachers, this has been widely seen to be a major element in their professional identity, and a major policy feature of the National Curriculum for initial teacher training:

> Got a lot to do with whether they like doing the subject and had the right training. (G-L-11)

> Some know their subjects better. (G-M-10)

> If teacher not doing own specialist subject, not so good. (G-U-7)

> Teachers who communicate well in lessons giving illustrations and examples, and know their subject better. (G-U-11)

Good teachers – what are we to make of the pupil perspective?

In summary, our analysis of the reasons which pupils gave for some teachers being better than others led to the construction and discussion of seven subcategories of explanation which were embedded in their responses. Table 3.6 reviews these and ranks them in order of importance.

When the weightings of the responses are broken down into these subcategories and ranked as they are in Table 3.6, we see how important is a teacher's interpersonal relationship with pupils, alongside the crucial ability to present and explain learning material and keep order in the classroom. The data throw light on the differences between the 'person' and 'task' orientation of teachers' roles. In particular, they point up the significance to pupils of their teachers' interpersonal posture and offer a detail to the associated skills which hitherto seems to us to have been underplayed in the discussion of teaching and training issues. Table 3.6 also summarizes the wide range of categories in which pupils make comments

Table 3.6 Why some teachers are better than others: summary ranking by category and percentage means

Category	% mean response	Rank
Teacher's interpersonal style or posture	28.6	1
To do with explanation and feedback	23.2	2
To do with methods of presentation	22.8	3
To do with classroom control and order	10.9	4
To do with how the teacher communicates	6.3	5
To do with miscellaneous reasons	5.6	6
To do with teacher expectations	2.6	7
Seven construct categories of reason	100	

about the quality of teaching and conveys the extent to which pupils perceive the many facets of a teacher's role.

Moreover, the pupils' detailed definitions of what they see as the good teaching requirements for their learning seem to us to mesh very closely with the most viable contemporary views on learning, such as that summarized, for example, by Bennett and Dunne (1994). These authors define learning as the extension, modification or elaboration of existing cognitive schemas, and remind us that there are tremendous variations in the schemata or knowledge of a topic held by children when they arrrive in any class. Children have schemata which are differentially complete or correct, and some of which are shared, and the child makes sense of teacher inputs by constructing links with prior knowledge, a process involving the generation, checking and restructuring of ideas in the light of those already held. Construction of meaning is a continuous process, and this view of learning is often referred to as 'constructivist'. Bennett and Dunne say that there is little argument among learning theorists that learning involves the construction of knowledge through experience, but that arguments occur about the conditions needed to optimize it. Should they be individual or social, children as 'social beings' or 'lone scientists', to cite Bruner and Haste (1987)? The now widely held social view given prominence by Vygotsky (1978) has led to an emphasis on negotiating and sharing in the construction of knowledge, so that a child's potential for learning is realized in interaction with more knowledgeable others. Central to the Vygotsky view is that through talk, inner (with themselves) and outer (within the class, the teacher and their peers), children organize their experiences into thought. The implication of all this, for Bennett and Dunne, is that teachers have to take children's individual, shared and idiosyncratic schemata into account in their planning of classroom tasks: the teacher has to be a diagnostician, eliciting and diagnosing children's conceptions, and then providing and presenting appropriate learning activities.

What the pupils across these ten schools said about good teaching and classroom practice clearly bears on all of this. In particular, their views on their requirements for both the social relations of learning and the varied learning activities to be presented to them by teachers would wholly accord with those of Bennett and Dunne on learning. Although they do not know it, these secondary school pupils are also Vygotskian!

We have frequently reiterated the point that pupils are capable of offering perceptive views about many aspects of classroom practice and that their voices could make an important contribution to the furtherance of appropriate pedagogies. We see the research evidence presented in this chapter as proof of that position. Our findings about good teaching mirror and extend those of earlier researchers such as: Woods (1979), Beynon (1985), Phelan *et al.* (1992), Lang (1993), Cooper and McIntyre (1995) and Rudduck (1996). We see our own contribution drawn from these pupil perspectives as filling out and significantly extending the earlier researches in respect of what pupils have to say about what happens in the classroom *per se*, rather than the whole range of school issues. However, regarding classroom practice, pupils and pedagogy, there is more to report in the next chapter, for the pupils in these ten schools answered questions about the quality of teaching and learning in addition to those we have discussed so far.

In this chapter, pupils send very clear messages about what constitutes good teaching. It pre-eminently is to do with the quality of the teacher's methods of presentation, range of learning activities, explanation and giving of feedback, classroom control and order, and interpersonal relationships. 'Quality teaching' for pupils is about activity, not passivity; about negotiation and close relationships, not distance and deference.

4 | Pupils and lessons: the best, the worst and those where they learn the most

In Chapter 3, we showed how detailed pupils' views are regarding their perceptions of the differences between good and not so good teaching. In order to explore further the whole topic of pupils and pedagogy, we asked them, as we indicated in Chapter 1, to reflect on what for them had been a 'best' and a 'worst' lesson, and to tell us in their own words what had made these lessons good or bad for them. In this chapter, we present and discuss how the pupils defined the constituents of their 'good' and 'bad lessons' experiences, and we also report how they rated eleven items which we presented to them in a written self-completion task entitled 'The lessons where I learn most are . . .'.

Characteristics of the 'best' lesson

Pupils were asked: 'Think of one of your *best* lessons since you have been at this school. What made it a *good* lesson for you?' Almost all could give us an answer by focusing in their recall on a good lesson experience (whether it had been the best or not), so we again wrote down what they said and analysed the 261 discrete segments of their statements for the essential meanings they contained, in the same way that we did for the pupils' answers about 'learning more' and 'good teachers'. The characteristics of the 'good' lesson which emerged produced essentially very similar re-sponse patterns (Table 4.1) to those which the pupils defined for 'good' teachers and 'good' teaching, as presented in Chapter 3 – as one might expect they should. We shall not offer here as many pupils' quotations, as they tend to duplicate those of Chapter 3.

Table 4.1 displays the main component categories of pupils' perceptions of the constituents of 'good lesson' experiences, together with the weight of response for each. It should be noted that whereas in Chapter 3 we included comments on 'control and order' within the main category of 'to do with classroom practice', in Table 4.1 pupil comments on control and

Table 4.1 Characteristics of the 'best' lesson: main categories of response ($n = 261$)

Main category	Mean % response across schools
To do with classroom practice, the actual process of teaching	53
To do with teacher–pupil relationships and classroom control	24
To do with how pupils relate to the subject being taught	23
Total	100

order are co-joined within the same category with those made on teacher–pupil relationships. The reason for this is that the pupil responses to the *best lesson* question invariably linked the existence of order with the ability to develop the relationship aspects positively. Control and order are self-evidently prerequisites for both the technical and relationship aspects of teaching.

'Best lessons' and classroom practice

The comments pupils made which have been put into this category in Table 4.1 relate to such classroom matters as: the teacher explaining effectively; effectively controlling the pace of the lesson; making the subject matter interesting; employing active learning; using practical and dramatic approaches; giving constructive help when needed by the pupil; and allowing pupils some freedom to work in their own way. Some examples of these were:

> History teacher explains really thoroughly, uses colourful words and is dramatic, and it's a bit more fun, we might do posters or write letters. (G-M-8)

> He gets through to you, puts jokes in and does dramatic things. (G-M-7)

> In French we play games – stepping stones going up a wall with a prize at the top so all get involved. (G-L-11)

> Science teacher took us down to the canal, we had nets and had to catch the insects and tested the water sample. (B-L-9)

> In English . . . *Treasure Island*, we had a film we discussed then wrote our own scripts in groups. (G-L-8)

> In German the teacher explains things deeply. We go around the room and say words. (B-M-8)

English, the way it was presented, explained well. (G-M-10)

In RE, we got a brilliant teacher, we do activities which are fun. (G-M-9)

We brought in a French picnic – you learn in a practical way. (G-M-9)

Best lessons: teacher–pupil relationships and classroom control

As with the perspectives on teacher–pupil relations which we have discussed in dealing with pupils' views of learning in Chapter 2 and good teaching in Chapter 3, the comments in this category here embrace the ability of teachers to foster positive interpersonal relations – whether they are friendly, kind and helpful to pupils, how they communicated with and encouraged them, or created a relaxed atmosphere with some fun and humour:

Teacher was friendly and regarded you as an equal almost, encouraged you to ask questions and didn't rush. (G-U-9)

Teacher kept everything under control behaviour wise and could discuss things at our level with humour. (B-M-10)

In science the teacher controlled the class so could concentrate on helping us, but not really telling us – guiding us. (G-M-10)

Maths teacher was nice, kind and helpful, made work enjoyable. (B-M-8)

While 77 per cent of pupils' explanations for their 'best' lesson experiences were attributed to the teacher's relationships or classroom methods, the reasons given on about one in five occasions were to do with the nature of the lesson's subject.

Best lessons: pupils and the subject

Comments in this category again parallel those we have presented earlier, and link learning or good teaching with the subject in some way:

Science – because I like doing experiments. (B-M-7)

Woodwork – something I wasn't all that good at but I made a love spoon. (G-U-10)

Whatever the appeal of the subject, it is wholly clear that overall it is the teachers who create the best lesson experiences by their enactment of methods, relationships and class control. All the quotations we gave above from answers about 'best lessons' parallel those made in answers about what constitutes 'good teaching'. 'Best lessons' for pupils are therefore very obviously the product of what the pupils defined as 'good teaching'!

Table 4.2 Characteristics of the 'worst' lesson: main categories of response ($n = 193$)

Main category	Mean % response across schools
To do with the way the subject was being taught and control in the classroom	39.5
To do with teacher–pupil relationships or the emotions and feelings of pupils in the 'bad lesson'	39.9
To do with how the pupil found the subject or topic	16.6
Miscellaneous reasons	4.0
Total	100

Characteristics of the 'worst' lesson

Pupils were also asked: 'Think of one of your *worst* lessons since you have been at this school. What made it a bad lesson for you?' In answer, about 5 per cent of pupils said there were no 'worst' lessons and that they enjoyed them all. But the majority were able to recall a bad lesson experience and articulate some reasons why it had been so. The answers to this question brought out virtually the same categories of meanings or explanations which we had received when pupils were characterizing the features of not so good and bad teachers and teaching, but with an interesting difference. Whereas previously they had been asked to focus on a source external to themselves, our question about a 'worst' lesson experience was essentially addressing how they internally felt about a lesson experience, and as a consequence it brought significantly more references to aspects of their own feelings than our earlier questions had revealed.

The constituents of 'worst' lessons are displayed in Table 4.2, these being divided into four subcategories. Equal in weighting, and together accounting for 80 per cent of all elements are pupil–teacher relationships (the affective dimension) and the way of teaching together with the quality of control (the technical dimension). The other two categories refer to issues to do with the subject being studied and 'other' reasons.

Worst lessons: the way the subject is taught

Remarks made under this heading confirm our earlier findings, namely that better teachers are judged to be so by their pupils because of the quality of their classroom practices. In the opposite case, 'bad' lessons are characterized by an absence of good teaching methods: poor presentation, the lack of practical learning activities, poor quality of explanation and feedback, and problems of classroom control and order. Some examples of these were:

> History, he just reads out of a book. (B-L-11)

> I like science but we never do any work and the teacher is always talking and then you have to work from the book. (G-M-8)

> French, there is so much writing to do, I don't understand it, and she doesn't explain. (B-M-9)

> In RE the teacher doesn't mark the stages and tells you to get on with the next but hasn't marked the work so that we can revise. (B-U-8)

> Everyone goes mad cheeking the teacher and then the teacher shouts. (B-M-9)

Worst lessons: teacher relations and pupil emotions

In analysing the 'best' and 'worst' lesson experience data to the point we have described here, we would have to say that the information has deepened, but not really added to, what we had already found out from pupils about the components of good classroom practice as they define it. With regard to teacher–pupil relationships, however, the 'good' and 'bad' lesson questions brought forth an additional dimension to the category of teacher–pupil relationships in quality teaching than we had so far derived from the earlier questions. The answers revealed important aspects of pupils' emotional feelings. For example:

> [Worst lesson] is where I am afraid, where the teacher has a feeling of superiority and you dare not answer a question for fear of being embarrassed or wrong. (G-M-12)

> I was blamed for something I didn't do and [teacher] made my life miserable thereafter. (B-U-12)

> In geography the teacher shouts. (G-L-8)

> French half of the time the teacher shouts and makes me unhappy. (G-M-7)

> There was not a proper teacher in English, he shouted at us when we asked for something. (B-M-7)

> Technology, the teacher made personal comments. (G-U-10)

> In maths I sometimes don't understand but I'm scared to put my hand up to ask. (G-U-8)

> Had to keep quiet and just get on with work, not sufficient explanation, felt you couldn't ask because you would feel stupid. (G-U-10)

It is absolutely clear by now that good relationships form an important plank in building quality teaching. This is not to say that the point in principle is startlingly new, but rather to indicate that an implementation gap persists between the rhetoric – what is desirable in providing a relational background for effective learning – and the frequent deficits in practice. It would seem that the relationship and emotional needs of pupils can be seriously under-appreciated, and that, even where they may be recognized, they require skills and strategies which may not be in the repertoire of many teachers.

Worst lessons: the subject

Just as some subjects are a positive 'turn-on' for some pupils, the same subject can be a 'turn-off' for others. We do not know why some subjects intrinsically appeal while others repel, and where we received passionate views to do with the subject, we were on many occasions unclear how far the interest perspective of the pupil had been mediated by teacher action or inaction.

> In maths do the same things all the time, just looking at numbers. (G-M-9)

> Art, because I don't like drawing. (B-L-7)

'Best' and 'worst' lessons: what do the pupils tell us?

We see three clear findings from this area of our enquiry with pupils. First, the characteristics of the 'bad' lesson are the obverse of 'good' lessons, a somewhat obvious conclusion. The second may not be so obvious: pupils across all schools consistently use the same set of characteristics to define good and bad lessons as they do to define good and bad teachers. Third, there is significant and important detail in the pupil view that highlights the repertoire of competencies which teachers should possess.

'The lessons in which I learn the most': what this written task told us

After the experience of listening to pupil answers to the core open-ended questions in the first two schools we visited early in our 'quality of learning' enquiry, we decided to include a written pupil completion part to the interview in subsequent schools. At the end of our oral interviews, therefore, pupils were presented on paper with a display of eleven items as shown in Figure 4.1. To answer the set task, pupils were given written instructions which required them to circle the appropriate number, and they were

The lessons in which I learn most are those where . . .

	Not important		Very important	
I like the teacher a lot	1	2	3	4
I like the subject a lot	1	2	3	4
We are made to work hard	1	2	3	4
We can have some fun	1	2	3	4
There is not too much mucking about	1	2	3	4
The teacher explains things really well	1	2	3	4
I am very good at the subject	1	2	3	4
I can work in a group with my friends	1	2	3	4
The teacher does most of the talking and explaining	1	2	3	4
I can find things out for myself	1	2	3	4

Figure 4.1 Pupil completion form: 'the lessons in which I learn the most'

advised that 'If you have any problems answering this question, the interviewer will talk you through it.'

We had devised this instrument as a means of seeking some corroboration of what the qualitative data was indicating at the time, and to test its potential for statistical manipulation in assessing whether there were any significant relationships in the patterns of response between genders, ages, ability groups or schools. The eleven items on the instrument are those we thought about in the very early months of what proved to be a five-year project. Had we then had sufficient qualitative data for analysis into categories in the way we have already presented, that analysis would have driven us to present to pupils a somewhat different list of items. We would certainly have included, for example, items along the lines of: 'where there are plenty of practical activities' or 'where the teacher is kind and very helpful'. But that is the sort of hindsight which is so apparent when the data are all in. Nevertheless, it is instructive to consider our findings from this self-completion instrument, because the information supplements the substantial picture of 'pupils and pedagogy' which the interview questions revealed.

Table 4.3 displays the rank order based on mean scores of the eleven 'lessons in which I learn most' items, which were completed by 156 pupils in eight schools. The items really divide between those which are something to do with the teacher's role, and those which are to do with certain

Table 4.3 'The lessons in which I learn most are those where . . .': rank order of pupils' responses by mean scores

Item	Mean score	Rank order
The teacher explains things really well	3.76	1
There is not too much mucking about	3.34	2
I like the subject a lot	3.29	3
I can find out things for myself	3.12	4
I like the teacher	3.10	5
We are made to work hard	3.04	6
I can work on my own in the subject	2.96	7
We can have some fun	2.90	8
I can work with friends	2.86	9
I am very good at the subject	2.84	10
Teacher does most of the talking	2.75	11

individual pupil preferences. The scores in Table 4.3 are based on the means of the numerical response positions the pupils had affirmed. Because the range of responses available was limited to 1–4, apparent small differences between the means are significant. Hence, the weight given to rank 1 (explanation) is really very significant indeed, and this holds true in importance for all subsets of pupils who completed the written instrument (Table 4.4). It also, of course, aligns with what the pupils said in their interviews.

Table 4.4 Self-completion instrument ($n = 156$): percentage of pupils by category ranking 'the teacher explains things really well' as 'very important'

Category of comparison	% 'very important' response
All pupil interviewees	80
All girls	81
All boys	80
Pupils in Years 7 & 8	80
Pupils in Years 10 & 11	82
Pupils designated lower ability	63
Pupils designated middle ability	84
Pupils designated upper ability	93

A clear majority of all pupils in all year and ability groups, and of both genders, designated the item 'the teacher explains things really well' as 'very important, producing its number 1 ranking with a very high mean score. Although the item referred solely to *explanation* in a teacher's delivery, we see it very much as a proxy for 'good' teaching methods as a whole, in the absence of other items to do with methods which, with hindsight, we would have liked to have included in the list.

The second ranked item ('there is not too much mucking about') is yet another endorsement by pupils of the importance of classroom 'control and order'. In the list of eleven items, we had included two – in ranks 3 and 10 in Table 4.3 – which are to do with the pupils' attachment to the subject as an explanation of 'learning most'. This was because at that time we were assuming this factor to carry a weight of importance which, as we have seen, was to prove significantly less when the interview answers came to be analysed.

As Table 4.3 indicates, 'I like the subject a lot' attains third rank position. We do not see this as really incompatible with the ethnographic evidence we presented in Chapter 2, where reasons to do with the subject accounted only for 7 per cent of all reasons given for explaining why they thought they learned more in some lessons than others. When the items below 'I like the subject a lot' in Table 4.3 are considered, these parallel factors which all had low weightings in pupils' interview answers, where so many classroom practice and teacher relationship elements dominated their comments. We are saying, then, that the relatively high ranking of 'liking the subject', was produced by this written exercise in the absence of 'competitor' classroom practice items which it faced in the interview situation, where the pupils determined the total list of items important to them.

We find the response in rank item 7 ('I can work on my own in the subject') interesting, in that while individual action was implied in many pupils' oral comments about lesson activities, it was not singled out in an explicit way. We see its middle ranking position here as conforming with pupils' interview statements valuing devolved learning activities, and underpinning to some extent the point we made earlier about ownership and pupil learning.

It can be seen that the scores in Table 4.3 fall fairly readily into about two halves: items with a mean score between 3 and 4 on the scale, reflecting a weight of 'important' and 'very important' response positions; and those between 2 and 3, 'the less important' and 'not important' responses. Of the first six items which have mean scores of 3 or greater, four of them (1, 2, 4 and 6) are predominantly in the area of the teacher's ordering of and control over the lesson. This aligns completely, as we have said, with the pupils' responses described in Chapter 2 about the main influence in their 'learning more'. But so too does the teacher item which is ranked bottom: 'teacher does most of the talking'. The teacher-dominated expository mode of pedagogy was deprecated in pupils' oral comments, so the position of this item produced by the written test is wholly congruent with that. The ways in which teachers do or do not make a difference as revealed by the written 'lessons in which I learn most' exercise therefore align with the priorities of what the pupils said in interviews. In the round, by the rankings in Table 4.3 the pupils are saying that, regarding 'learning',

Table 4.5 Self-completion instrument ($n = 156$): levels of agreement between categories of respondent on 'the lessons in which I learn most'

Category of comparison	Correlation coefficients*
Between schools	+0.54 to +8.0
Between boys and girls	+0.88
Between Years 7 & 8 and Years 10 to 12	+0.70
Between lower and upper ability groups	+0.63

* These are calculated using Spearman's rank order correlation coefficient (rho).

teacher performance takes precedence over their own perceived abilities or likings. Now, to what extent is this response pattern consistent across schools, between the genders, between the ability groups and across the year groups?

We subjected the data to detailed statistical analysis and found that, taking the schools as a whole, and whatever the differences between their settings, which we explained at the beginning of this book, there is a high level of agreement between their pupils about the priorities accorded to the items we posed in the self-completion question (Table 4.5). As Table 4.5 shows, the rankings produced in the eight schools correlated with each other in a range that is indicative of a high level of agreement between pupils irrespective of school. We also considered the other subsets within the totality of the pupils who completed the written exercise.

We considered: potential gender differences, differences arising from age and year group in the school and, finally, ability levels. Of course, these three aspects are not necessarily independent of each other. A girl, for example, may respond in two quite different ways to the items, depending upon whether she is at the start of her secondary career or moving towards GCSEs. When we calculated the correspondence of the rankings of the items across all schools for girls and boys, we established a rank order correlation of +0.88, a very high level indeed (Table 4.5). There was also a similar positive and very substantial correlation between the priorities of boys and girls, and their age and ability groups. By this test, and as was the case with the interview data, boys and girls have similar priorities regarding pedagogy, whatever their age or ability.

We also examined whether the pupils' perceptions of the elements of classroom processes and interrelationships presented to them in the self-completion question differ between the year groups by constructing three categories of comparison: the combined Years 7 and 8 (which arguably represents the time for pupils of peak novelty with respect to secondary school and the way that it works), for Year 9 (the year of transition, when many pupils are midway between entry to and exit from the school) and for Years 10 and above, three stages which cross-link with pupils' physical and sexual changes, and their curricular move to an external examination

Table 4.6 Self-completion instrument ($n = 156$): pupil age group intercorrelations on 'the lessons in which I learn most'

	Year group	
Year group	9	10–12
7–8	+0.71	+0.70
9		+0.84

focus. In Table 4.6, we display the correlations we obtained, and again the pattern is one of agreement at a high level.

This corroborates what we found with our interview data, and is a significant finding. It has been a widely held view that teachers have different relations with pupils in Years 7 and 8 and pupils in Years 10 and beyond, and need different skills to cope with these different age groups. The change according to year group has been described, for example, as from where, in Years 7 and 8, teachers are under pressure to motivate pupils by providing work which is intrinsically interesting, to where, in Years 10 and 11, teachers are urging pupils to focus on good grades and strategies for examination success (Rudduck 1996: 58). There is no evidence from our interviews or from the results of the written self-completion exercise that pupils from the lower and higher year groups perceive their pedagogic needs in different ways. Indeed, the evidence is clear-cut. Pupils of all ages have the same generic priorities for what they require from their secondary school teachers.

A third line of evaluation we made statistically was to assess whether the prioritizing of the eleven items presented to pupils varied according to the *ability group* designation the schools had given our pupil interviewees. We found there to be substantial agreement between the three ability groups, but there were some minor distinctions between the lower ability group and the upper and middle ability subsets. The three ability groups gave similar priority to 'teacher explanation' and 'mucking about', and the upper and middle ability subsets had virtually the same priorities across their rankings of all items. However, lower ability pupils ranked 'we can have some fun' and 'we are made to work hard' significantly lower than their higher ability peers. While the perspectives of lower ability pupils do conform with those of all other pupils regarding desired teacher pedagogies as a whole, we have here, as we found with the aspect of 'control' and lower ability that we discussed in Chapter 2, some subtle distinctions related to lower ability pupils. Clearly, there is scope here for follow-up research regarding the detail of the learning and teaching needs of these pupils.

Overall, this mechanistic measure we made of items to do with lessons where pupils learn most revealed a consistent pupil profile of priorities for good teaching and learning, a profile which was very similar for children of both sexes and all ages and abilities in the comprehensive school. Within that profile, it is the items to do with teachers' classroom actions which are prioritized, and, of these, two stand out in the pupils' ratings: the lessons where pupils say they learn most are where 'the teacher explains things really well' and 'there is not too much mucking about'. This is, of course, entirely consistent with the much richer and detailed qualitative data which we obtained from the interviews.

Pupils and pedagogy

In this chapter we have presented the pupil perspectives we obtained when we asked them about their 'best' and 'worst' lessons and, via a written exercise, the lessons where they learn most. We see there to be three prime features to what the pupils said about pedagogy which extend and confirm the perspectives we described in Chapter 3: the importance of the practical teaching skills to do with presentation, explanation and range of learning activities; the importance of relationship skills in communication, setting the social climate of learning in the classroom and supporting the individual pupil's emotional needs; and the overall importance of enacting a balance between the practical or technical aspects of teaching and the affective or relationship aspects of the teacher's role.

At the time of preparing this book in early 1998, the government in Britain was reiterating pronouncements about teachers' pedagogy. The use of more traditional methods so as to ensure basic number skills in the teaching of mathematics in primary schools was to become a policy priority, and the acquisition of traditional teaching skills in teacher training would be emphasized. In the various trumpetings of these 'new' policy directions, there was a rhetoric that these changes derived from what research had shown. We are clear about neither what this research base is, nor the definitions of 'traditional' the government is adopting. What we are clear about, though, from this and other research revealing pupils' definitions of good pedagogy, is that issues of teaching quality are too complex and subtle to be reduced to policy standpoints based on dichotomous value positions, and that there is a clear need for what the pupils say to have influence on policy discussion.

We have shown in chapters 2, 3 and 4 that pupils really do know what they think constitutes good teaching, and that they voice in their own ways the same precepts of best practice which expert trainers and teachers acknowledge. In fact, we would say the same thing about our pupil interviewees from British comprehensive schools that Phelan *et al.* (1992) said regarding students on another continent, namely that their views concur with what contemporary learning theorists and cognitive scientists have to say about optimal instructional strategies. They prefer an active to a passive role; they prefer transaction to transmission; and they want to learn through a range of activities. In addition to a clear preference for dynamic pedagogy, they favour teachers who are willing and able to assist them in understanding the material, who have the oral skills and will take the time to explain concepts and ideas carefully and thoroughly, and who demonstrate a commitment to help them learn. While this seems an obvious compilation of the qualities of a good teacher, in what we reported in this and the previous two chapters, the pupils in essence are asking: why cannot all teaching match these criteria?

The message of this chapter is that pupils are consistent in their definitions of the constituents of good teaching, whether these are given freely in interview answers or constrained by the choices presented to them in a paper and pencil test.

5 | Teachers and pupil learning: why some learn better than others

We had asked pupils about the reasons why they thought they learned more in some lessons than others as a means of revealing the factors they thought important to their learning, and we discussed these in Chapter 2. When we interviewed a selection of the teachers who taught these pupils in all but one of the ten schools, we similarly wanted to know from them what factors they saw contributing to the ways in which pupils learn. We asked them: 'To what do you attribute differences in the rate at which pupils learn – that some pupils learn better than others?'

In all, 133 teachers answered this question, and we wrote down their responses, which ranged from simple sentences in the majority of cases to more complex paragraphs of opinion, and analysed them for discrete statements of meaning which we categorized. Altogether, we found that we could separate out 337 discrete reason statements. Most of them offered more than one reason in the totality of what they said, but very strangely one teacher could see no differences at all in the rates at which pupils learned.

We analysed the teachers' responses for their essential meanings, and found that in the first place we could put them into one or other of four main categories of reason. The teachers said that some pupils learn better than others because of: 'something to do with the pupil or his or her home background'; 'something to do with me, the teacher; 'something to do with the nature of the subject'; or 'other reasons'. There was a very clear-cut pattern to the teachers' reasons why pupils learned differently (Table 5.1), and in many ways the categories were parallel to those produced by the pupils' answers to their question about learning (Chapter 2, Table 2.2).

Across the schools as a whole, the category of reasons which were 'something to do with the pupil or his or her home background' constituted a massive 62 per cent of all the separate response statements given. We should note that this constitutes an interesting parallel and contrast with what the pupils said on the topic in Chapter 2 (Table 2.2). Both the teachers and the pupils allocated about 60 per cent of their reasons to one category, and the weightings are similar for the other three categories. In Table 5.1, the balance of the teachers' weightings given to the respective contributions of the 'pupil', on the one hand, and of 'me, the teacher', on the other, to pupils' learning better is the exact opposite of that we received from the pupil perspective. The pupils themselves see teachers as making the overwhelming contribution to their learning, whereas teachers perceive that the differences are massively related to the pupils themselves; they just don't seem to see how vital they are to the learning process. We shall take up this and other matters of comparison between pupil and teacher perspectives in Chapter 7.

Table 5.1 Why some pupils learn better than others: teachers' main categories of reasons ($n = 337$)

Response category	*Mean % responses across all schools*
Something to do with the pupil or home background	62
Something to do with me, the teacher	18
Something to do with nature of subject	9
Other reasons	11
Total	100

The major categories of response pattern shown in Table 5.1 for schools as a whole was in fact consistent across the nine schools, and the weight given to this category was consistent across all schools (Table 5.2). Table 5.2 shows that in all the schools where we interviewed teachers, the rank order of the main categories of response is very much the same. Teachers,

Table 5.2 Why some pupils learn better than others: variation across schools in main response categories (percentage response)

School	*The pupil*	*The teacher*	*The subject*	*Other*
A	81	14	0	5
B		No data collected		
C	62	22	6	10
D	58	21	9	12
E	72	6	16	9
F	58	16	16	16
G	70	18	0	12
H	67	15	9	9
I	52	25	8	11
J	69	9	11	10
Mean	62	18	9	11

as a whole, share the same perspectives regarding why some pupils learn better than others in whatever type of school they teach, whether the school, on the basis of the percentage of pupils achieving five or more good grade passes at GCSE, is a high performing school such as D or E, or one of those in the bottom quartile of the performance league such as H or I. Similarly, comparable proportions emerge whether teachers are in a large urban comprehensive with neighbourhood catchment area, such as school C, or one located in a small town with a much wider catchment area, such as I.

As we explained in Chapter 1, we interviewed different numbers of teachers in the schools, these varying in terms of length of teaching service, the subjects they taught and any wider responsibilities they held. Therefore, alhough we had not matched their profiles between school and school, the patterns of response to our question on pupils' learning turned out to be the same. It seems clear, therefore, that we have a generic view on this topic, irrespective of teacher identity or the social and demographic context of a particular school. We shall consider later why this should be so, after describing the categories in more detail, and indicating the subcategories within them of the reasons teachers give to explain pupils' differential learning ability.

Learning better: something to do with the pupil

From what we had recorded of the teachers' replies to our question, we had allocated to this category 211 'spoken reason statements', which referred in some way or another to an attribute connected to the pupil in explanation of why some learned better than others. There were four subcategories making up these pupil-related comments (Table 5.3), three of which can broadly be described as dealing with psychological or personality factors related to pupils. There was a fourth category, of more sociological

Table 5.3 'Pupils learning better than others': something to do with the pupils or their home background ($n = 211$)

Subcategory	Mean % response across all schools
To do with the individual pupil's psychological attributes, i.e. intelligence, motivation, concentration	32.9
To do with a pupil's cognitive competences, i.e. attainment in basic and other skills	8.9
To do with other personality features of pupils	3.26
To do with sociological attributes: parental influence and home background	17.5
Total mean % response	62.56

or social features relating to the pupils' home and community situations. In their replies to us, the teachers did not, of course, use terms such as 'psychological' or 'sociological' – these are our constructions, intended as umbrella labels to encompass the reasons or attributes they spoke about in their everyday language. In the examples of what the teachers said, which we now go on to give, we think that it will be self-evident why we have used these terms. Later, we shall be arguing that the main explanations which teachers use for the differences in pupils' learning can be connected with certain ideologies in their training background and school cultures, within which psychological and sociological frameworks have dominated.

Learning better: the 'psychological/personality' reasons teachers offer

These cover the first three subcategories displayed in Table 5.3, and they are, in common parlance, to do with certain ability components of personality with which individuals are endowed, competences which they have attained and can be relied on to perform or a range of other personal or personality features which are believed to be idiosyncratically connected with a pupil's learning achievement.

Pupils' psychological attributes

The predominant group of reasons which teachers give to explain why some pupils learn better than others embraces statements dealing with 'intelligence' and 'ability', 'motivation' or 'concentration and ability to pay attention', which are subjects or concerns of the formal academic discipline of psychology. As Table 5.3 shows, such *psychological attributes* as these constitute about a third of all the different reasons given which are 'to do with the pupil', and constitute the largest of the seven subcategories into which the teachers' responses as a whole can be distributed.

In using the term *intelligence* we are, of course, here taking our cue from the language used by the teachers themselves rather than entering the complexities of the concept as it is analysed in standard psychology texts. For some teachers, it was sufficient only to refer to differences in learning in these terms. In the illustrations of what teachers said, which follow, we indicate in parentheses the author's professional identity. *Gender* is shown by 'M' or 'F'; *length of service* in years by one of three categories (1–10, 11–20 or 20 + years); and *professional status*, where CT stands for an interviewee who was essentially a class teacher, HOD/HOY shows a head of department or head of year and SM indicates a member of senior management such as a deputy head (SM).

Some children have more intelligence than others. (M/11–20/CT)

A greater ability to understand. (M/20+/HOD)

Different abilities and talents. (F/1–10/CT)

Intellectual ability. (F/11–20/CT)

Academic nature from birth. (M/20+/HOD)

Grasp things in a different way – spatial awareness, for example. (M/20+/HOD)

Here, for the most part, teachers are talking about intelligence/ability attributes in a broad, perhaps even intuitive way, one that is hardly distinguishable from the discourse of everyday life. In general, 'intelligence', as can be seen from this selection of quotations, where it is qualified, might be 'basic', 'innate', 'natural', 'inherited'. Refinements of the term – for example, whether it is immutable or capable of development – were almost wholly missing.

A quarter of all responses which teachers give for some pupils learning better than others is related to what is seen to be innate intelligence or ability. The implication is that this is a given, determinate factor, and, as we shall discuss, taken in the context of their responses as a whole, there may also be an implication here that teachers feel that they have little or no control over this factor. 'You can't teach intelligence' has been a strongly held viewpoint, originating, as we shall argue, from earlier formulations of the concept.

The presence or absence of what our teacher interviewees called *motivation* was another important reason they gave for pupils' learning differences. This accounted for more than one in ten of the factors put forward under the major construct of things to do with the pupil. As with intelligence, this was often stated, sometimes as part of a checklist, baldly and without elaboration:

Ability, motivation . . . (M/1–10/CT)

Nearly two-thirds of the teachers citing motivation stopped at that point, giving no indication of whether motivation was of the same order, for example, as their view of intelligence; that is, whether it was a quality already possessed by the pupil or whether they meant that the pupil found difficulty in becoming motivated despite the teacher's efforts. However, the use of terms such as 'self-motivation' and 'personal motivation' gives us a strong hint that the teachers are construing the concept in the first of these two ways. For example, and more elaborately, it was put to us that:

Some are more willing to work, others are lazy. (F/1–10/CT)

Some are more self-motivated. (M/11–20/HOD)

It's the lack of motivation of the children that is their problem, not their ability. (F/20+/CT)

Motivation. If they want to, whatever their ability, they will make progress. (F/20+/HOD)

Teachers saw the lack of motivation as lying with the pupils themselves, for in only two cases was it said that motivation was influenced by other factors, such as the part they, the teachers, might play.

> It is the motivation and the enthusiasm of the teacher. (M/20+/HOD)

> Motivation – part of this is the responsibility of the teacher. (M/1–10/CT)

It can be seen from the statements by teachers that a key aspect of their notion of *motivation* is that pupils *are not* motivated – that it is not a quality that they possess, or that it has been lost somewhere along the way. That is, they see the pupils as not bringing with them into the classroom the quality of eagerness to learn and to sustain an interest in the tasks with which they are presented. It further implies that there is within pupils a 'capacity of motivation' in much the same way that there is a perceived general ability or intelligence. The main inference that we draw from our data, then, is that teachers very largely see *motivation* as something with which pupils are endowed or not. Typically, they will say that 'pupils aren't motivated' and, just as in the case of intelligence and ability, the majority of their observations in this category are simply made baldly. On the evidence of their statements, only a very small minority of teachers recognize that they have a part to play in the process of motivating.

Closely related to the previous category were teacher observations on pupils' level of concentration or ability to pay attention to their work. These accounted for about 10 per cent of the reasons to do with the pupil in teachers' explaining why some pupils learn better than others. For the most part, the point was put in terms of a capacity which the pupil lacked. For example:

> Some haven't the ability to listen and concentrate. (F/11–20/CT)

> Some pupils have a longer concentration span. (F/11–20/CT)

> Their concentration span is the main thing. (F/1–10/CT)

> Their innate ability means that some have better concentration spans. (F/1–10/CT)

> Powers of concentration. It is a growing problem – they suffer from the sound-bite syndrome. (F/20+/HOD)

Again, for the most part, teachers' statements on concentration indicate that they view a pupil's capacity for concentration as a quality within the pupil, either possessed by him or her, or more usually lacking or deficient. It would probably be generally recognized that most people do have some restrictions in respect of periods of uniform methods of learning, but that this can be made more effective by attention to the internal organization of extended time spans. The pupils themselves recognize this when they reject, for example, lessons which are entirely given over to exposition and passive learning. It follows that the capacity of concentration is, or should be, intimately tied in with the activities of the teachers – not only in the quality of the teaching material, but also in the substructure of lessons. Moreover, concentration on a task can reasonably be considered to be a skill, and therefore one that can be learned alongside other study methods. A recognition of the teacher's role in relation to pupils' concentration, and of the fact that concentration has a dynamic element and therefore can be affected by factors both within and beyond the pupils themselves, was conveyed in the statements of only very few of our teacher interviewees:

> Their concentration span – affected by the planning of lessons and who they sit by. (F/1–10/HOD)

> Learning is affected by their ability to listen and concentrate and some of this down to me. (M/10–20/CT)

> Children may not have developed the means of concentrating. (F/1–10/CT)

As with the *psychological* attributes of intelligence/ability and motivation so far discussed, the implication of teachers' remarks is that *concentration* is seen in somewhat 'concrete' terms, that it is a quality which pupils *have* rather than one which can be nurtured and developed as part of their armoury of learning skills. The learning environment within which concentration is to take place or the nature of tasks to which concentration is supposed to be applied is acknowledged by only a very small number of the teachers.

Pupils' cognitive competences

Teachers mentioned the lack of certain cognitive competences in some pupils as another reason why they did not learn as well as others. These reasons were to do with either competences that should have been, but were not, achieved prior to arriving at the comprehensive school, or the absence of certain general basic skills. In particular, they pointed to significant differences in pupils' attainment in the basic skills, especially reading, which they saw as attributable to what had taken place in the earlier years of schooling in the feeder primary schools. Examples of what they said include:

> How the subject was introduced in the primary school – it varies between the schools. (F/20+/SM)

> Their ability to read affects their performance in the subject. (M/1–10/CT)

> What they have done before they have come to us. (F/11–20/HOD)

> It's their basic skills. They don't know their tables. (F/1–10/CT)

Differences in the feeder schools – there are some basic skills lacking. (M/1–10/CT)

Pre-secondary school learning – reading and writing skills are paramount. (M/1–10/HOD)

Sometimes the judgement about the quality of pre-secondary achievements is put in the context of the reading age of pupils, in which a standard test had been used to assess the pupil's level. In all other cases, such as those cited above, the implication was of a general impressionistic judgement being made about shortfalls from earlier education, with no reference being made to any information derived from SAT achievements. The important point which we take from these observations is that, in teachers' perceptions, the lack of certain basic skills constitutes another constraint upon pupils' learning, which, by implication, is in many respects beyond their control.

The more general assertions about lack of a suitable cognitive basis include:

Difficulties in language skills. (M/11–20/CT)

Aptitude in maths. (F/11–20/CT)

Pupils' confidence in music. (F/11–20/HOD)

Maths is based on numerical skills and literacy. (F/11–20/CT)

Again, these comments almost imply that prior learning is in some ways not adequate to the challenges of the secondary school curriculum, although one head of physics indicated that the problem existed in a different form:

Confidence in maths is a basic in physics, but the National Curriculum is not helping. For example, we make use of vectors, but the maths curriculum is not related to ours – needs more coherence. (M/11–20/HOD)

Other personality features

About 20 per cent of all the pupil-related factors which teachers gave to account for differences in pupils' learning were essentially related to some aspect of a pupil's general character or personality, and these could be very varied. One teacher mentioned 'problems with the birth process', another the age group, while (general) confidence and self-reliance, innate personality, physical make-up and stamina and, finally, pupils' self-perceptions occurred a couple of times each. Examples of these sorts of statements are:

Their self-confidence. (F/20+/DH)

Self-reliance. (M/20+/CT)

Levels of self-confidence – pupils have to stand in front of the drama class. (M/1–10/CT)

The perceptual reality of their life. (F/11–20/HOD)

Age group of the child – their qualities. (F/20+/CT)

Their physical make-up. (F/11–20/HOD)

It will be obvious that a more miscellaneous category of statements such as these contain meanings which are difficult to assess. 'Personality' in its colloquial usage embraces views on general traits which are often idiosyncratically perceived through pupils' actions and responses to the more concrete aspects of their lives.

Nevertheless, we find in them echoes of a general psychological paradigm shaping teachers' views of learning, which is reflected, as we shall argue, in one of the main streams of teacher training. Here, we would want to note that, in invoking of 'other personality features' alongside 'cognitive competences' and 'psychological attributes' as explanations of pupils' learning differences, there is implied something of a deterministic set on the part of teachers.

Pupils' sociological attributes

Of all the pupil-related factors that we discuss in this chapter, pupils' home background assumes great significance to teachers, having almost equal weighting with teachers' judgements of pupils' intelligence or ability in explaining differential learning. References to home circumstances constituted a quarter of pupil-related attributes according to the teachers we interviewed. For the most part, they make this point in one of two ways. They refer to home background *in general* – about a third of all references are to this factor – or their comments speak about *parental support* – about a half of background factors. Examples of the 'general' comments are:

Their home circumstances. (F/1–10/CT)

Their home environment. (F/20+/HOD)

Their parents. (M/1–10/CT)

The family background. (F/20+/HOY)

The pupils' cultural background – social things and behaviour. (F/1–10/CT)

On one or two occasions only is this developed. For example, one teacher added a remark about the material circumstances of the home (how important it was to have a table on which to work), while another referred more generally to:

Facilities at home which encourage children to do the homework. (M/1–10/CT)

Invariably, the statements were bald, and only rarely was the core reason being expressed or developed further, so that *home background in general* was seen as conducive, or more usually detrimental, to effective learning in the classroom.

Teachers referred in similar manner to parental support. Elaboration of the point only occasionally makes explicit whether this support is for the pupil or the school, although most statements in this category imply a pupil-oriented construct of parental support:

Parental encouragement is important for learning. (M/1–10/CT)

Those who do it on their own and those who are well supported by parents. (F/11–20/CT)

The quality of parental support . . . even those who exert pressure on us for extra work. (F/1–10/CT)

Support from home – only some complete the homework. (F/20+/ CT)

Problem homes where children do not complete the work. (F/1–10/ CT)

Good life parents who don't turn up for evenings – they don't reply to communications – they are unconcerned. (M/11–20/SM)

Teachers' 'other' comments mentioned a particular aspect of the pupil's home or pointed to the ethos or values of the home as a relevant factor when considering the effectiveness of pupils' learning.

Parental support – some have a different set of values. (M/1–10/CT)

Home background – some have a better work ethos. (M/11–20/CT)

We have described these home background and parental support reasons which teachers offer in explanation of why some pupils learn better than others under the general term of 'sociological attributes', as we see them as linked to the other influential, *sociological* ideology of teacher training in recent decades, and we shall discuss this after we have described all the categories of answers the teachers gave to our question.

Learning better: something to do with me, the teacher

Out of the total of 337 discrete reason statements we received from teachers, only 60 (or 18 per cent of the total) were to do with their own role as teachers in the context of some pupils learning better than others. We should recall here that the total of 337 reason statements were provided by 133 teacher interviewees, so that, on average, each individual offered

Table 5.4 'Pupils learning better than others': something to do with me, the teacher (*n* = 60)

Subcategory	Mean % response across all schools
To do with teaching methods	13
To do with teacher–pupil relationships	5
Total mean % response	18

between two and three factors. Yet teachers 'wrote in' a distinctly subordinate influence for themselves.

There were 83 teachers or 63 per cent of our interviewees who did not cite a reason relating the effectiveness of pupils' learning with their own role in the classroom. Moreover, there is wide variation in the proportions of teachers from the individual schools who seem to discount their own work. In schools E and J, 81 and 80 per cent respectively of the teachers interviewed did not write themselves into the reasons given for some pupils learning better, while in schools C and I there were 45 and 40 per cent respectively who did not.

It is not easy to account for this wide variance, but it may be an artefact of the different mixes of teacher interviewees we received from school to school, and we would readily acknowledge that had we directly asked all teachers something like 'what is your role in the differing learning achievements of pupils', all of them would have included themselves, perhaps even giving a quite detailed account. However, the key point here is that the majority of teachers did not immediately include themselves among the reasons why some pupils learn better than others.

The factors which were put forward by teachers concerning their own role in pupils' learning, could be divided, as Table 5.4 displays, into teaching methods in general and teacher–pupil relations. Against the background of all factors, these account respectively for about one-eighth and one-twentieth of the total of 337 factors, and within the major category the balance of teaching methods to teacher–pupil relationships is of the order of 2.5:1.

Learning better: teachers and teaching methods

The teachers gave three clusters of reasons in relation to their teaching methods and pupils' learning. They were to do with: teaching at the right level and pace; using interesting presentation and varied methods; and having good aims, presentation and motivating strategies. The most frequently mentioned factor (36 per cent of statements to do with teaching) was teaching at the right level and pace for the pupil. For example:

Work must be pitched at the right level for them. (F/20+/CT)

The ability of the teacher to teach to individual levels. (F/1–10/CT)

With a wide ability range, you have to use a lot of different strategies. (M/1–10/CT)

Quality of teaching: resources, the accessibility and appropriateness of the material. (M/20+/SM)

Children are different. The way that they are taught may not recognize those differences. (F/20+/SM)

There is in statements like these a clear awareness of the different capacities of pupils, and this accords with the high emphasis placed upon pupils' ability which we discussed earlier, although the teachers do not for the most part offer any criteria by which they differentiated their approaches.

Second in frequency within this subcategory, at about a 30 per cent frequency level, is the more general need for teachers to make their subjects more interesting to pupils. Like the first cluster of comments, this can also involve the need for differentiating their teaching strategies.

Best to give all pupils as many opportunities as possible. (M/11–20/CT)

I try lots of different strategies regarding the materials but there is less scope for experimentation in English [nowadays]. (F/11–20/CT)

Differences in learning style. Children like a variety of methods – some may prefer group work. (M/1–10/CT)

You have to catch their interest immediately. (F/11–20/HOD)

The third cluster of factors (18 per cent) acknowledges that teachers have an explicit function to enact good preparation, clear aims and a commitment to motivate pupils:

You need to be very well prepared – right levels and for different abilities. (F/11–20/HOY)

Clarity of aims and targets in lessons. (M/20+/CT)

The enthusiasm of teachers is important. (M/20+/HOD)

Using different methods to motivate and stimulate them. (M/20+/HOY)

Motivation – if you can spark them off. (F/1–10/CT)

Motivation is part the teacher's responsibility. (M/1–10/CT)

The remaining comments covered such aspects as creating an appropriate classroom environment, the teacher's self-discipline and general agreement that some of the reasons why some pupils learned better than others were 'down to the teacher'.

Given the significance of teaching methods in all teacher training courses, the relatively low emphasis (in terms of their frequency of occurrence) placed upon teaching methods here is interesting, but perhaps not surprising in the light of the overwhelming significance to our teacher interviewees of pupil characteristics and home circumstances. Does this mean that they consider matters of pedagogy relatively powerless in the face of these other factors; that they perceive their own actions in influencing pupils' success at school as relatively weak when set against the 'psychological' and 'sociological' attributes of the pupils who turn up from their school's catchment area? We take up these questions later.

Learning better: teacher–pupil relationships

Table 5.4 shows that only 5 per cent of the total reasons given by teachers refer to teacher–pupil relationships as a factor in pupils' learning. Even within the 'to do with me, the teacher' subcategory, the issue of teacher–pupil relations accounts for fewer than a third of the total teacher-related reasons. Essentially, the teachers' comments referred in general terms to the desideratum of good teacher–pupil relationships without specifying what the required components of good relationships with pupils for learning purposes are. For example:

The relationship between teacher and child. (F/11–20/SM)

Pupils finding an affinity with the teacher. (F/1–10/CT)

Otherwise, in terms of relationships with pupils, this category included fairly eclectic reasons along the lines of 'personality of the teacher', 'importance of making eye contact with pupils', 'pupils liking the teacher' or 'teachers knowing the class'. Overall, we find that teachers have surprisingly little to say about connecting teacher–pupil relationships with better learning.

The expansion of the teacher's role in modern times, to include a strong emphasis upon pastoral matters, and the pressure to take on social work tasks, especially for pupils who experience one or more of the many forms of deprivation, has been a constant theme in the discussion of teachers' roles. One important element of such tasks as these is, precisely, the establishing of strong relationships, and pronouncements of the caring nature of the profession are part of the currency of educational debate. Indeed, suggestions that the caring part of the role has got out of hand are not unusual. One of the head teachers in the ten schools, a relatively new appointment, told us that his intention was to shift the culture of the school away from an overemphasis upon the pastoral and towards a greater degree of achievement orientation. But, he added, he was meeting stiff resistance from many of his established staff.

So what are we to make of the fact that pupil relationships are much more concerned with *caring* in the general pastoral sense, than with *learning* in the cognitive achievement sense, so that little connection is made between pedagogic strategies and relationship skills? This is an issue we shall take up in Chapter 7, where we compare pupil and teacher perspectives.

Learning better: the nature of the subject

As Table 5.1 indicates, teachers also saw 'interest in' and 'liking for the subject' as a reason for some pupils learning better than others, and this category constituted 9 per cent of all teachers' reasons. Again, in looking at what the teachers said, it is necessary to distinguish between those who *catalogue* factors which seem to them important in accounting for different rates of learning and those who place the idea of interest in some wider context. Indeed, it was interesting that some responses did imply a list where the interviewees were, so to speak, checking off the points on their fingers. With respect, first, to the catalogue type of response, the majority of comments in this category did in fact simply list 'interest in the subject' as an important factor. Others, however, place the same theme in broader or other contexts:

> Success in the subject breeds success. (M/20+/CT)

> Some pupils are sportingly inclined – we provide a broad spectrum of sports for them here. (M/11–20/HOD)

> Their enjoyment of the subject. (M/11–20/CT)

> Confidence in music. (F/11–20/HOD)

> Their interest in the subject which comes from the personality of the teacher. (M/1–10/CT)

We think that 'interest in' and 'liking for the subject' is both a product of pupils' own disposition towards an area of knowledge and derived from teachers' methods and enthusiasm. Both the pupil and the teacher response linking 'the subject' to learning appear to be at a significantly lower level than is generally assumed to be the case.

Learning better: other reasons

Teachers also gave reasons which were to do with something other than 'the pupil', 'themselves as teachers' or 'the nature of the subject' in answer to our question about why some pupils learned better than others, and this final category accounted for about 11 per cent of all response reasons (Table 5.1) and covered a variety of matters. Chief among these 'other' reasons were comments about the way pupils were grouped for teaching purposes; that is, whether teachers saw banding, setting or mixed

ability grouping affecting pupils' learning. The views expressed often implied a value position:

> Lower ability children are not being pulled. (M/20+/CT)

> Material will not stimulate the less bright pupils. Need to mix able
> and weak pupils together. (F/11–20/CT)

> Differentiation not welcomed by children. (F/1–10/CT)

> Whether groups are structured in such a way that facilitates progress-
> ive pupils. (F/20+/CT)

Other issues covered in this 'other' reasons category were: aspects of general school organization, e.g. 'able children will get more help at parents
evenings' (F/1–10/CT); age of individual pupils within the year group,
this referring to the debate about varying advantages conferred on children born at different times of the year; the diet pupils have; who pupils
sit by, and influences of the peer group generally; gender matters, e.g.
'Girls are prepared to learn while boys mature more slowly', 'Older girls
who are more sexually aware become more easily distracted' or 'Boy–girl
rivalry'; and the occasional diffuse or odd comment such as: 'different
perceptions of life' or 'problems during the birth process'. Such comments as these were relatively insignificant in number, and we do not
think that they make any important contribution to the overall discussion,
but it was perhaps surprising that the issues of peer group activities and of
gender differences did not, in fact, form a stronger strand in the teachers'
accounts.

Just as we did for pupils, having analysed what the teachers said, we
considered whether there were types of reasons to account for pupils'
differential learning which were not expressed by teachers but which might
have been expected. We received no comment from teachers that class
size was a factor, though this had been cited by pupils. Only two teachers
referred to a link between resources and pupils' learning, though this
matter was a topic of hot debate during the period we were undertaking
the research behind this book.

Learning better: determinism and process factors in the teachers' perspectives

We observed earlier that teachers 'wrote themselves into' the answers to
our question about pupils learning at a subordinate level, and we now take
this issue further by considering how much teacher control over the learning process is implied by their answers to the question we posed. We shall
also offer an explanation of the level at which teachers placed the contribution of their own role so consistently across the schools where we
interviewed them.

Table 5.5 'Pupils learning better than others': response categories and contribution of teacher (*n* = 133)

	Percentage response
Respondents omitting the teacher's role (n = 84)	
To do with the pupil only	45
To do with the pupil and something else	15
To do with something else only	3
Total %	63
Respondents including teacher's role (n = 49)	
To do with the teacher alone	4
To do with the teacher and the pupil	23
To do with the teacher and something else	1
To do with the teacher, the pupil and something else	9
Total %	37
Overall total %	100

First, we need to obtain a closer fix on the level of teachers' response which invoked themselves. Up to now, our analysis has been made in terms of discussing the relative weightings of the 337 discrete reason segment statements which we separated out of teachers' responses, but this did not tell us how many individual teachers gave replies that in some part of the answer contained one or more segments invoking their own role. Table 5.5 shows the proportion of teachers who made some explanatory reference to themselves in the main categories of response we discussed earlier. As a measure of the extent to which individual teachers see some role for themselves in pupils' differential learning, we looked at the totality of individual teachers' responses, and assessed whether they 'wrote themselves in' in terms of three categories. On this occasion, the 'something else' category embraces data we included in Table 5.1 under 'other' and 'the subject'.

Table 5.5 shows the frequency with which one, more than one or all three categories of response were incorporated into their replies. Only about one in ten of the teachers interviewed perceived the effectiveness of pupils' learning to result from the interplay of all three main categories of reason. In the largest category, 45 per cent of individual teachers gave responses which were only 'to do with the pupil', and a further 18 per cent of individual respondents gave a reply which made no reference to their own role.

This means that 63 per cent of teachers excluded themselves from the equation, as it were, so that only a minority – four out of every ten teachers – see themselves as having some part in pupils' differential learning. This level, however, is higher and more valid than that which was suggested by an earlier measure in Table 5.1. There the measure involved the absolute number of teacher-related comments per category within the totality of answers rather than individual people. We stress that we take such measures as these to be indicative of teachers' general perspectives on the issue posed, rather than accurate calibrations. However, whether we take either measure or both, we think they give a reflection of how teachers perceive their own level of influence within the totality of factors causing some pupils to learn better than others. That is, they see themselves as playing a decidedly subordinate part in influencing learning compared with other factors: those to do with the pupil, the subject or other reasons they described to us. In particular, the level expressed for their own influence is very modest compared with the psychological and sociological attributes that teachers say pupils bring with them into the classroom. The main question arising, therefore, is why this should be so.

In attempting to resolve this issue we are aware, of course, of a number of possibilities. For example, the frequent public denigration of teachers which has taken place over recent years undoubtedly will have led to some loss of confidence. Nevertheless, we think that the answer is essentially to do with the extent to which, on the one hand, teachers believe the scope for learning is largely determined for them, or on the other, the influence they believe they have over the pupils' learning through their own teaching processes.

Determinism, process factors, ideologies and teachers' perceptions of learning

In this context, *determinism* is taken to be, from the perceptions of the teachers, factors which are given, fixed and largely beyond their control. *Process factors* refer to the interrelationship between the teacher's professional skills and the pupil as learner, and constitute an essentially dynamic construct. For example, in terms of the reasons teachers expressed in answer to the question discussed in this chapter, the 'home circumstances' of the pupils can be construed as largely beyond the control of teachers, as would be pupils' prior learning experiences at primary school. On the other hand, all aspects of the process of teaching, teaching at the appropriate level for pupils' ability, for example, is a matter within the teachers' powers to affect. In terms of the data we have displayed and discussed in this chapter, we can evaluate the various categories as to whether they are *deterministic* or *process* in status.

The status of the majority of them, such as those we have labelled as pupils' psychological and sociological attributes or those to do with the teacher, is obvious. We also needed to assign the other and sometimes more ambiguous reasons which teachers gave for some pupils learning better than others to a *deterministic* or *process* category. To take, for example, the pupil's diet or the school's policy on setting or mixed ability, we saw these offered as reasons beyond their control. When we totalled the two categories, with allowances made for possible mixed status positions in respect of 'motivation' or 'the peer group', say, we found a clear preponderance of deterministic factors, with the process factors not much above 20 per cent of the total.

Again, we do not see this as an exact measure, but it is indicative of how, broadly, teachers see the challenge of teaching and learning as containing constraints beyond their control. We argue in Chapter 8 that this is a perspective which in the current context of knowledge about learning potential, as well as societal needs for the twenty-first century, radically requires addressing. Here we wish to offer an explanation as to why this perspective is as it is.

Since the Second World War, there have been a number of distinctive ideologies that have permeated teacher training which, we believe, will have had a bearing upon the perceptions of teachers about their pupils' learning potential in the classroom. These ideologies received greater emphasis as teacher training courses become more 'academic', as courses lengthened from the emergency training courses immediately post-war through to two and later three years, culminating in the four-year BEd courses, before recent changes brought a reduction to three- and two-year BEd courses again.

We think the teacher perspectives on pupil learning we have discussed in this chapter need to be considered against the broader context of teacher training during the past fifty years. We see the ideologies of teacher training which have prevailed as causative of the level of deterministic beliefs exhibited by our teacher interviewees, whatever entry route into teaching they have followed. The balance of the training syllabus during this period progressively shifted away from the practical issues of classroom teaching towards first psychological and later sociological studies as the setting for dominant pedagogical ideologies.

For about the first decade and a half after the war, educational psychology formed the keystone of courses about children. This had two broad effects. First, there was a growing emphasis upon child-centredness in the curriculum, whereby children's developmental stages were considered paramount in judging what levels of tasks were appropriate for each age group. This reached an apogee in the theoretical work of Piaget and in the related educational policies emanating from the Plowden Report. Although the latter was concerned with primary education, it was a powerful influence on the training (and trainers) of teachers in the late 1960s and 1970s. It strongly reinforced the idea of the child as a natural and inquisitive learner and the teacher's role as keeper of the greenhouse. Provided that ambient conditions were appropriate, children would 'naturally' flower into maturity. In both respects, the message as interpreted by teacher trainers and their students was that there were limits, or at least a predetermined order, to the scope of educational advancement experienced by the children at any one stage in their development.

Second (and in the present context more significant) was a heavy emphasis upon the measurement of intelligence, which had dominated educational research in the early part of the century. This emphasis was so great that the tripartite structure of education following the 1944 Education Act was premised not only upon the normally distributed intelligence quotient (IQ), but also upon the 'discovery' of a number of recognizable aptitudes. The essential truth about intelligence, as far as teachers at this time understood, was that it was a natural phenomenon, that it could be measured and that it was not susceptible to cultural or subcultural differences in children's backgrounds. As far as teachers were concerned, this *psychometric* ideology meant that ability or intelligence, the raw material with which they worked, was a factor beyond their control. It was a given quality, determined at birth.

Towards the end of the 1950s, systematic research studies gave birth to another ideology, which indicated that achievement in school, far from being a straightforward consequence of levels of measured intelligence, was, in fact, closely related to the child's social background. The higher the social class, the greater the likelihood of reaching a higher standard. In its early formulation, this new ideological strand might have pointed to factors about school curriculum and processes which could be construed as inimical to certain socioeconomic groups, but in fact two important influences combined to reinforce a deterministic attitude on the part of teachers.

The first was that, in exploring the *mechanisms or processes* by which social class affected the achievements of pupils, the idea arose that language ability could restrict working-class pupils' access to, and engagement with, the demands of education. Second, and partly as a development from this type of research, Marxist ideologies also gave a more deterministic impetus. This resulted from an emphasis upon the notion that schooling was a means of controlling and socializing the large majority of pupils into a social system that was essentially alienative, in the sense that the majority of working-class pupils, with the exception of a small proportion of 'sponsored' individuals, were unable to benefit from the education system. In short, there was some sort of opposition or conflict between schooling and the needs and perception of the working classes.

We would therefore see the teacher perspectives on pupils' learning which we have discussed in this chapter as heavily influenced by these two ideologies which have permeated teacher training: the *psychometric* and the *sociological.*

Countervailing ideologies have, in our view, been very weak or absent in teacher training. In more academic quarters in this period, more process ideologies were establishing themselves. There were the notions that *charismatic* leadership through school headships together with dedicated staff could make exceptional achievements; the emerging management studies ideas which pointed up that schools can bring about effects beyond the expectations suggested by their environment; and, most recently, the emergence of learning research demonstrating the benefit of transactive methods and the recognition of different types of learners.

However, the persistence of the influence of the two principal deterministic ideologies in teacher training is, we believe, reflected in our analysis of teachers' responses to the question about differences in the rates at which pupils learn. What is particularly interesting is the fact that the pattern of responses did not vary in any significant way with a teacher's length of service. The views of the younger teachers, with five years service or less, were as *deterministic* as the views of those who had been in the profession for twenty years or more. It would seem that either their more recent training has maintained the status quo in terms of the ideologies transmitted, or the influence of staffroom subcultures had triumphed over the more contemporary ideas regarding learning and ability to which they were introduced in their more recent training.

We do not know which of these is the more true. Either way, the teachers' perspectives on ability, intelligence and motivation, and the relationship of these to children's learning, appear to us to be very undifferentiated and 'frozen' in out-of-date states of knowledge, in the belief patterns which were held relevant earlier in the twentieth century rather than in what are available to educators from the scientific knowledge available as we approach the end of the millennium.

We would observe that the perspective revealed on intelligence or ability – that it is something fixed and decidedly limiting, a view which has been described as the 'single minded, single funnelled approach to the mind' (Gardner 1994: 44) – needs to be revised by embracing the notions of multiple intelligences and differing learning styles. The work of Howard Gardner has demonstrated seven types of intelligence: logical-mathematical, linguistic, spatial, kinaesthetic, musical, interpersonal, intrapersonal. Only two of these are object free. The other five depend on relationships with the external physical world. Gardner argues that this state of affairs has important ramifications for instruction. Teachers must recognize the manifold ways individuals can exhibit this range of intelligences so that many talents are not overlooked. Their teaching methods need to reflect these multiple intelligences by translating knowledge and problems from one intelligence domain to another if they are to achieve optimum success.

There are other theoretical positions to do with the differentiated nature of pupils' abilities, which could revise the ideologies driving teachers' classroom practices. For example, Kolb (1983) and others have argued the importance of individual learning style. In Kolb's case, there are four styles: *activists*, who learn best from short here-and-now tasks, and learn less well from situations involving a passive role; *reflectors*, who learn best from activities where they are able to stand back, listen and observe, and learn less well where they are rushed into things; *theorists*, who learn best when they can review things in terms of a system, concept, model or theory, and learn less well from activities presented without this kind of explicit or implicit design; and *pragmatists*, who learn best where there is an obvious link between the subject matter and concrete problems in real world situations, and learn less well from learning events which seem distant from their own reality and which do not seem to apply to their situation. There are two key points, as we see them, about contemporary knowledge of human intelligence and differing styles of learning. First, these factors are no longer viewed in the deterministic light in which our teacher interviewees appeared to see them; second, the contemporary views declare malleability regarding ability, so that the pupil is open to the process skills of the teacher.

A similar revision to teachers' learning ideologies is required regarding their beliefs on motivation. Research in recent decades has derived educationally relevant conceptions of motivation which have much to say about the connection between motivation and intelligence, and motivation and optimum learning and the associated teaching strategies. Dwech (1986) and research associates, for example, have shown from their studies that *motivation*, or the causes of goal-oriented activity, involves two classes of goals: *performance* goals, in which individuals seek to gain favourable judgements of their competence or avoid negative judgements of their competence; and *learning* goals, in which individuals seek to understand or master something new. The crucial part of these researches is that children who believe that intelligence is a fixed trait tend to orient towards gaining favourable judgements by way of performance goals, with progess built around children's concerns with their ability. Children who believe that intelligence is a malleable quality will orient towards developing *learning* goals, where there is a focus on progress and mastery through effort. These views imply a distinction between what Dwech calls *entity* theory – a theory of intelligence as fixed – and *incremental* theory – which sees intelligence as malleable. The researches show that, when teachers take the entity/performance goals perspective, children focus on ability judgements and there is a tendency for them to withdraw from challenge. On the other hand, where teachers' work is driven by an incremental/learning goals perspective, children focus on progress through effort, tend to seek out and be energized by challenge and are willing to risk displays of ignorance in order to acquire skills and knowledge. These researchers assert that retraining children's attributions for failure away from the notion of ability and towards effort has produced sizable changes in persistence in the face of failure, changes that remain over time and generalize across tasks.

The main conclusions that we draw from teachers' answers to our apparently uncomplicated – almost naive – question is that teachers believe they have but a small amount of influence over pupil learning, a view which is consistent whatever their length of service, subjects taught, gender or type of role held within the school. They essentially had a 'single funnel' view of intelligence and an 'entity' view of motivation, and we see there to be a clear cultural lag in teachers' ideologies or beliefs about the potential of pupils' learning. If these findings are correct, they are important, because the beliefs about ability, motivation and the potential for achievement which teachers transmit to their pupils are crucial for the individual's esteem and self-actualization and the future of the country in the global economy and information society. In saying all this, we do not wish to imply any fault on the part of teachers, for if there is this deficit regarding ideologies of learning, as we think this research demonstrates, the reason for it must clearly be laid on the desk of government. Policies for teachers' in-service development over recent years have given no priority to generic pedagogy and learning issues. Nor do teachers in the UK, unlike teachers in some advanced countries, have designated professional development programes and sabbatical leave as of right. We return to this issue in Chapter 8.

In this chapter, the message from teachers is that 'good learning' very largely derives from the endowed innate abilities and the attitudes pupils bring with them from their parental environment; teachers see the quality of pupils' learning as connected only in a very modest way with their own behaviour.

6 | Teachers and pedagogy: views of their own teaching

In Chapter 5, we showed that, when questioned directly about differences in pupils' learning, teachers underplayed the significance of their own professional role. But what happens when the attention of teachers focuses more upon matters of pedagogy? Do factors to do with their own role in the classroom play a more prominent part? Two broad issues are raised by this question. The first is whether teachers characterize a particular approach to their classroom work. The second, and more important one in the present context, concerns the actual principles which, they say, guide their teaching strategies.

We explored these pedagogical issues by putting to our teacher interviewees two specific questions. In this chapter, we discuss the responses we received to these questions and draw out some general conclusions about teachers' views on pedagogy. We posed our first question within the context of certain polarities frequent in public debate: *'We hear a good deal these days about traditional and progressive methods of teaching. Do you have an identifiable style of teaching and, if so, what is it?'* As with all other questions we have so far analysed, we noted down what they said and analysed their responses to discover the embedded definitions, descriptions, and reasons which the teachers offered.

Teachers and 'styles' of teaching

The terms 'traditional' and 'progressive', when applied to teaching methods, are not of themselves very helpful in pinpointing typical pedagogical stances adopted by teachers, since there is a general lack of clarity about what each entails. This diffuseness has been aggravated by the fact that the terms have been taken into public discourse about educational issues and in particular as education becomes a progressively sensitive political issue. This has conferred upon them a somewhat spurious concreteness and a public consensus about their meanings. As if that were not enough, the

Table 6.1 How teachers defined their 'style' or general approach to teaching (*n* = 99)

Category of response	% in category
Traditional	20
Mixed but tending towards traditional	18
Mixed	56
Mixed but tending towards progressive	2
Progressive	4
Total	100

term 'progressive' has attracted a strong pejorative connotation, repres-enting at the lowest level, for many outside education, an attack upon teachers who have a tendency to 'forget the basics' and become 'ideo-logically doctrinaire' in their delivery of the curriculum.

Nevertheless, we framed the question in the way we did so as to key the teachers in to the nature of the topic and to give an opportunity for interviewees to talk about their style of teaching as different from, or con-gruent with, these 'polar' terms. In fact, none of the interviewees directly challenged this formulation or complained that the terms constituted an oversimplification of a complex process. Could it be that they are profes-sionally adept at handling questions which are posed in arguably naive ways about the classrooom? Whatever the case, we shall show that, by their responses, these secondary school teachers gave evidence of being far more pragmatic and traditional in their approach to delivering the curriculum than would have been thought from listening to a good deal of public debate or the popular press.

In Table 6.1, we show the distribution of the teachers' declared styles in terms of five categories, ranging from 'wholly traditional' to 'progressive', and there are some initial points to be made about the construction of this table. The first is that with about 15 per cent of the responses received it was not possible to allocate a style with confidence to any of the five types. For example, if the respondent gave as an answer: 'my style is a good relationship with the pupils', this could reasonably have been attrib-uted to any of the five types we had constructed from all answers. We have therefore not counted such replies as these in Table 6.1. Nevertheless, we noted such responses and have included them in our subsequent analysis of the data.

The second and key point about the construction of the five categories shown in Table 6.1 is that teacher responses frequently qualified one of the polarity positions by replies embracing 'a tendency towards' position. Hence, 'a tendency towards tradional' or 'a tendency towards progressive' response, together with a modal or 'mixed' response position on the part of the respondent, gave us our five categories.

It will be noticed that, in Table 6.1, the number of teachers contributing to the data, i.e. 99, is fewer than the 133 who contributed the data on pupils' learning discussed in Chapter 5. This is because the question about characterizing teacher style was not put in some schools (or to all teachers in the others), as we were obliged to complete our interviews within a framework of the wider topics for investigation determined by the individual schools and their timetables. It was not always possible to ask every scheduled question, particularly if this meant discourteously restricting teachers' responses to the earlier questions about the topic of special interest to that school. Where we put this question and received responses, we found that we could place teachers into one of these five categories of 'teaching style', and one-fifth of them gave an unqualified description of themselves as 'traditional'.

In the discussion which follows, we cite, as we did in Chapter 5, the 'teachers' voices' on the topic.

> Chalk and talk – I cannot leave them to discover for themselves – they can find out untrue things. (F/20+/HOD)

> Traditional – I place a big emphasis upon set ways of learning – I'm teacher orientated, skills need repetition. (M/11–20/HOD)

> I am a bit of a disciplinarian. When I talk, the pupils don't. (M/20+/ HOD)

> Traditional, mainly talk and chalk. I do some group work though. (M/11–20/HOD)

> Traditional – tend to whole class teaching, and use of blackboard. I have experimented, but progress more with traditional. (M/20+/CT)

> In business studies, traditional. I introduce the subject, read from a book, ask questions, then mark and go over them. (F/1–10/CT)

> Traditional, lot of standing up and board work, and use of text books, but some discussion. (M/1–10/CT)

> Traditional – starts with me talking about the topic and then giving them some notes and some examples. (M/1–10/CT)

Clearly, the word 'traditional' resonated with some teachers, but as the above citations show, there was a range of surrogate terms in operation. Words like 'formal' and 'didactic', 'chalk and talk', 'whole class teaching' and 'running a tight ship' all signify a more teacher-directed approach to pedagogy. In the extreme, traditional methods imply maximum teacher control over the learning process and an unwillingness to allow for any pupil ownership of teaching and learning strategies. The danger of learning untrue things referred to by one respondent amply illustrates this. It can be seen from the citations above that declarations of a 'traditional' style of teaching were made by teachers from each of the 'length of service' categories, so that this style is not one connected with an older generation of teachers. In fact, the last two citations in the above list were made by males who had been in teaching for less than five years.

Others, while indicating variety in their approaches, nevertheless saw themselves as traditional in tendency:

> Borders on the formal, I need to be in control – they all listen unless I say carry on. But anything for variety. (F/20+/SM)

> It varies according to the nature of the topic but [I am] getting back more to didactic, because if you don't, they don't learn. (F/1–10/CT)

> I try a variety [of approaches] but I am more traditional than I like to think I am. I make an effort to do flexible learning. (M/1–10/CT)

Of those from whom we received reasonably categoric answers about their style of teaching, a clear majority wanted to describe themselves in a mixed position regarding the polarities presented to them in the question:

> Mixture. I fit methods according to the circumstances, fit them to the groups being taught. (F/1–10/HOD)

> Use a mixture, any sensible teacher does this – it would be easier to have them in front of you in a formal setting. (F/11–20/CT)

> Fair mix adapted to nature of the class. (F/1–10/CT)

> Depends on the topic. I'm traditional for some but pupil led for others. (M/1–10/CT)

> I adapt to the topic. A good teacher will use the strengths of both. (M/20+/HOD)

> I mix and vary my approach. We are encouraged towards the traditional here, but I try to take into account individual difference. (F/20+/CT)

Only a minority of responses were in the 'tending towards progressive' or clear-cut 'progressive' categories, and the term 'progressive' was used very infrequently in the teachers' statements we allocated to these categories. We allocated largely on the basis of our summation of their responses based on cues such as references to child-centred, the individual or clear non-traditional aspects of classroom practice.

> Trying hard to be progressive but we teach grammar here. We need more variety, encourage pupils to speak. (F/20+/CT)

> I try to adapt the method to the class but, in general, I am more progressive. (M/1–10/CT)

> I'm non-traditional [in that] I involve the pupils – pass the responsibility to them. (F/11–20/HOD)

> I use child-centred approaches – role play, individual, paired and group work. (F/11–20/CT)

> Really good preparation is essential [and] a knowledge of the children, what makes the individual child tick. My style is informal, special needs teaching often is – very personal and interactive. (M/20+/HOD)

Examples of statements we found difficult to classify and which are not covered in the table are:

> Where kids are at. Pitch lesson about right. You need to be well organized and capture their imagination. (M/20+/CT)

> Try to get rapport with the kids – get them enthused. I can only do this with firm discipline. (M/20+/CT)

In terms of the five categories of teachers' styles of teaching, the clear majority of teachers declare some type of mixed style, which should come as a surprise only to those who set out to demonize teachers by suggesting that the profession is dominated by 'progressive' ideologues. If anything, the only surprise to us in the responses was the number declaring themselves as traditionalists. Among these, as some of the citations above illustrated, there seemed to be a belief that traditional methods are associated with pupils' best progress and learning achievement, and this raises again for us the issue of how teachers might have access to reliable empirical knowledge in respect of the connections between particular classroom methods and demonstrated learning achievements.

Although we were able to derive some picture of the distribution of declared teacher styles, what really characterized teachers' answers to this question more than any other we asked of either pupils or teachers was an astonishing diversity in the terms and criteria that the teachers used to elaborate their approach to teaching. The range of constructs offered varied enormously – and in our 'first pass' notings, when we began to allocate categorizations, we produced far more than for any other question that we put to pupils or teachers throughout the series of interviews. What this diversity of response reflects, in our view, is that there is a substantial lack of homogeneity in the vocabulary and concepts available to teachers with which they are able to describe their teaching activities and the factors that drive them. In fact, when we posed the question about 'identifiable style' in our interviews, our common experience was for teachers more to hesitate somewhat and search for something to say rather than have ready answers about their own teaching. By their demeanour and the content of what they said, it seemed that teaching methods were something they enacted rather than thought about a great deal, or analysed in any systematic way.

In the answers to our question about style, the 99 teachers gave us 108 separate explanatory statements in amplification of their overall pedagogical stance: traditional, mixed etc. We analysed these in terms of what

Table 6.2 Focuses of pedagogy in discussing style of teaching ($n = 108$)

Focus category	Focuses	% in category
Teaching methods	Use of group work Exposition stage to lesson Problem-solving activities	31
Relating method to pupils	Varying approach to level of pupil Child/pupil-centred Need to stimulate/involve	31
On the teacher	Teacher's control and order Teacher-centred	21

To do with the subject	Teaching approach varies
	  with subject
	Need for repetition of certain
	  subject skills
		11

Relationships	About pupil–teacher relationships	6

aspects concerned these teachers; that is, the essential topic focuses of their responses to the question about teaching style. Table 6.2 shows that the elements of pedagogic role which concern teachers in discussing their style of teaching could be allocated to one or other of five categories. As might be expected, the clear majority of teachers' comments, 62 per cent, were concerned in some way or another with teaching methods, and were equally divided between those directly on methods and those to do with relating methods to the children in some way.

Focus on teaching methods

By 'focus', in this context, we simply mean what the teachers say they characteristically *did* to organize lessons and teach them. It accords closely to what Cooper and McIntyre (1995) call the *technical* aspect of their role, as opposed to their observations about the climate in which they taught. The most frequently mentioned element *within* this category is the use of group work as part of the lesson, which, together with the second element about an exposition stage to the lesson, accounts for over three-quarters of the category as a whole.

Pupils respond well in groups on practical methods. (F/20+/SM)

I divide them into groups to investigate a problem. (F/20+/CT)

Teach from the front when necessary but also break down into groups. (M/20+/HOY)

Second in frequency teachers referred to the inclusion of an introductory expository stage in their presentation of a lesson:

> I first explain the theme to pupils and then tell them what to do. (F/20+/CT)

> It starts with me talking about a topic and then getting them to take notes. (M/1–10/CT)

The other 25 per cent of responses in this focus on methods category included: instigating problem-solving, class learning, mixed ability teaching and the inclusion of a practical element in the lesson.

Focus on relating methods to pupils

As Table 6.2 shows, this category equals the first in frequency. The most common way in which teachers put the point – accounting for more than 60 per cent of elements within the category – is in terms of teachers varying their methods of teaching according to the ability level of the pupil:

> Depends on the nature of the group. With the better ones it's chalk and talk, but I can relax with the lower groups. (M/1–10/CT)

> It's a mixture of methods, depending on the groups. Some can respond to a more formal approach, but with the less able I am less formal. (F/11–20/CT)

> I adapt by trial and error to the type of students. I now use a wider range of methods – more like a primary school. (M/1–10/CT)

> I am tougher on brighter children but teach middle band pupils in a middle band way. (M/20+/HOY)

Another element within this category related directly to pupil or child-oriented methods, and makes up a further quarter of cited factors:

> I'm pupil-centred. I use a mixture of methods – could be group, individual worksheets, etc. (M/11–20/SM)

> I involve the children – they need to be physically active. (F/11–20/HOD)

> You need to know what makes the child tick. (M/20+/HOD)

> I try to challenge them to take a wider view than just following step-by-step, sometimes it's open-ended. (F/20+/HOD)

The need to stimulate was also mentioned within the ambit of this focus upon the pupils and methods:

I'm traditional but will use any gimmick to attract pupils' interest. (M/11–20/HOD)

I need enthusiasm from the children. I try to catch their imagination and desire to debate by asking extra questions. I am a traditionalist, it's the way I function. For me that is successful. (F/11–20/HOD)

I instil enthusiasm with well structured lessons – good aims and objectives. (M/11–20/HOD)

An interesting feature associated with those quotations which refer to the need for differentiating teaching methods according to pupils' ability is that higher achievers should receive more formal teaching. The apparent reasons for this, in an ethos of the primacy of examination and other test results, hardly need rehearsing. More important, however, is the implication that if the curriculum is to be efficiently delivered to the pupil (within the given constraints of range of subject content, of time scales and of a regime of periodic testing), then more didactic methods are demanded. We compare this perspective in Chaper 7 with pupil views of teaching methods and their relationship, if any, with ability categorizations.

Focus on me, the teacher

Comments we included in this category were those that conveyed a focus either on classroom control and order, or on 'me, the teacher' being in charge. Strictness and control in lessons was the predominant idea being expressed in this category, and makes up nearly 90 per cent of teachers' responses within it:

I have to have good class discipline – with every child busy and working. (F/20+/CT)

You can't rely entirely on group work – there has to be control. (F/10+/CT)

Have a particular style to create a stable environment. (M/20+/HOD)

There has to be tight discipline in drama. (F/11–20/HOF)

The climate is set by the teacher. They need to be prepared and ordered – having objectives with changes in lessons if needed. I like an orderly atmosphere – you cannot work if there is disruption. (F/11–20/CT)

The weight of teachers' responses with respect to the need for a disciplined and orderly classroom is of particular interest in the light of what the pupils said about teacher control in answers to the question about good teaching. Judged by the absolute number of comments made by teachers on 'control and order', it would appear to be of significant concern.

However, this is misleading, for if the aspect of classroom order is related to the absolute number of teachers who refer to it, rather than the proportion of this category in teachers' comments as a whole, then the picture is very different. Fewer than one in five teachers (19 per cent) remark on the need for an ordered classroom environment. It may, of course, be argued that this is a taken-for-granted factor, that it 'goes without saying'. Nevertheless, the overwhelming majority of the teachers interviewed had other, more significant (to them) elements to advance in describing their style or approaches to teaching.

The other 10 per cent of statements falling in this focus category have been labelled 'teacher-centred', and these statements assert the centrality of the teacher, such as: 'I am teacher-based – directive' (F/1–10/CT).

Focus on requirements of the subject

References to the subject itself and to the need to develop and practise certain subject relevant skills define this category:

> Need a knowledge of the subject to decide on the general approach to teaching it. (M/11–20/HOY)

> The subject requires me to deal with the curriculum in a way that uses a lot of individual work sheets. (M/11–20/HOD)

> I adapt my way of teaching to the topic or subject – a good teacher uses both methods. (M/20+/SM)

> I do oral drilling – it is an essential part of language teaching. (F/1–10/CT)

> Basic skills in languages need constant repetition. (M/1–10/HOD)

> Every child follows the same spelling lists – it does them good to learn as a class. (F/20+/HOD)

Again, it is interesting that reference to the subject is relatively infrequent, with little more than one in ten of all comments referring to links between subject and delivery. Even in those cases where teachers drew attention to the connection, their responses did not elucidate any generic principles to differentiate teaching approaches to the substance of the curriculum. Otherwise, reference to the subject is only a means of contextualizing their accounts.

Focus on relationships

This category of teachers' pedagogic concerns has the lowest weighting and is therefore concordant with what we have reported regarding the priority teachers give to the affective aspects of classroom role:

I try to get an individual rapport with the kids. (M/20+/CT)

I admire the traditional methods but having youth on my side, I try to build up relationships. (M/1–10/CT)

Personal relationships with the pupil are very important. (F/1–10/CT)

Teacher–pupil relationships account for only 6 per cent of total responses, and the significant factor here, as with 'classroom order and control', is that there is a divergence between pupils' and teachers' priorities, an issue we take up again in Chapter 7, where teachers' and pupils' perspectives are compared.

In putting the first of our questions about pedagogy to the teachers, we had hoped to obtain some measure of the extent to which they ascribed to themselves a definite teaching style and the elements of classroom practice they would connect with it. We have seen that in describing their teaching styles, a wide range and diversity of comments characterized the teachers' responses. But on the whole these were fewer and less detailed than the pupils' responses to the question about pedagogy. This may have been the consequence of the way this particular question was posed, or a reflection that teachers rarely discuss such matters as styles of teaching and methods. We had, however, planned another doorway to teachers' views about pedagogy in asking a second question to them about lessons.

Teachers and the 'specially good' lesson

The second question relating to pedagogy was put to 120 teacher interviewees: *'Think of a specially good lesson that you have given recently – when you came from the classroom and thought "that lesson went excellently". What were the factors that contributed to it being a good one?'* One of the teachers was unable to call to mind a lesson which fulfilled the requirements, and therefore the following analysis is based upon a total of 119 teachers. They were, of course, drawn from across the entire subject range indicated in Table 1.5.

It was intended by this and the previous question about teaching styles to give teachers the opportunity for a progressive refinement of their perspectives on pedagogy – from the general sweep of teaching styles to the elaboration of principles driving a particular lesson. In order, therefore, to give a sharp focus to the question, we followed it up by stressing that the selected lesson should have been 'out of the ordinary', one that had 'hit the button': 'when you ended that lesson, you felt that something special had happened'.

We intended that teachers' responses might reveal how they connected success in a lesson with their own pedagogy. Although the same question was asked in a similar way to all the teacher interviewees, inviting them to describe an exceptional event, only a minority answered the question directly, for they treated it in three different ways. The majority, i.e. 61 (or 51 per cent) of the teachers, did not refer to a single specially good lesson, but spoke only in terms of successful lessons in general. Fifty-three interviewees (44 per cent) did respond by referring to a defined special lesson, while a third group of six interviewees (5 per cent) gave responses which combined comments on a special lesson and good lessons in general.

It seemed curious to us that over half the teachers were unable to recall a special lesson, and chose rather to discuss 'good lessons' in general, and it is difficult to decide what the significance of this is. In most professional work, peaks emerge from the plateaux of everyday working life – otherwise life becomes very humdrum, and an important source of reward and inspiration is not experienced. Perhaps this situation reflects the fact that no formal methods are generally used to gauge the success of a particular lesson, so that special success is dependent on an exceptional or charismatic type of experience which a majority have just not had within recent recall. Whatever may be the case, at the time, we did not challenge our respondents that they were not answering as requested, but noted down and later analysed what they had said in their own terms.

Given three different types of response to this key question, an immediate concern was whether there would be significant differences in the three subsets of replies. Analysis of the responses from the 'special lesson' subgroup and the 'successful lessons in general' subgroup revealed no significant differences in response patterns. Nor were there any relative differences between these two and the small mixed subgroup, so in our analysis we treated the data as a whole however the interviewee had interpreted the question. In the discussion of findings which follows, we ignore these three subgroups, and discuss this topic area of special or good lessons under the generic heading of *successful lessons*.

Teachers' definitions of successful lessons

From the teachers' responses it was possible to derive a total of 246 reason statements about their successful lessons. As Table 6.3 displays, teachers explained their 'successful' lessons in terms of: 'to do (in the main) with observed pupil responses', 'to do with methods of teaching' and 'other factors'. These categories represent the terms in which the teachers themselves defined successful lessons and delineated the relevant factors which they saw as contributing to them.

Table 6.3 shows that more than half the responses were concerned, precisely, with the ways they saw that pupils had responded in the 'successful' lessons they could bring within their recall in answering our question. Success factors attributable more directly to their own professional skills in constructing and teaching lessons took second place in the weight of their comments. In a sense, therefore, teachers are here saying more about the

Table 6.3 Teachers' perceptions of the constituents of
successful lessons ($n = 246$)

Category	%
To do with observed pupil responses	51
To do with 'my' methods of teaching	35
Other factors	14
Total	100

pupils' capacity for learning than they are about their own practice, and
we take this as further evidence of the point we made in Chapter 5, that
teachers tend to underplay their own professional contribution.

Successful lessons: observed pupil responses

Within this main category of responses to explain successful lessons,
teachers' reasons could be divided into *affective* and *technical* subcategories
(Table 6.4).

Table 6.4 Successful lessons and observed pupil responses ($n = 126$)

Subcategory	%
Pupils participate, respond positively, show interest, are motivated, interact with the teacher etc.	36
Pupils have learned, have been extended, have developed	15
Total %	51

Pupil response and 'affective' factors

The more important of these two, which might be called the *affective*,
connotes elements such as pupils' demonstration of enjoyment, a positive
response in terms of involvement in tasks and expressions of motivation
and interest. The second refers more directly to learning that had been
accomplished by the pupils – a *technical* or *instrumental* element, signifying
a more direct outcome with respect to intended learning. Where observed
pupil responses are concerned, therefore, the teachers we interviewed are
more inclined by a ratio greater than 2:1 to point to the former, the affective elements, as criteria for judging that a lesson went well. The following
are examples of teacher statements in this subcategory:

> The way that the pupils listened. You could see on their faces that
> they enjoyed the lesson. (F/20+/HOY)

When they are involved and task-orientated. (F/1–10/CT)

The responsiveness of children. There was maximum participation and the activity was done with enjoyment. (M/11–20/HOD)

It was a project lesson. There was a high level of participation and responsiveness to what I am doing. I try to give them self-belief. (M/1–10/CT)

Children were involved with the task and understood about the intended end product – what we were trying to achieve. (F/1–10/CT)

Pupils were all involved – everyone seemed to get something out of the lesson. (M/11–20/HOD)

It will be clear from the above examples that teachers refer to a range of affective aspects in their observed pupils' behaviour as indices of pupil engagement, learning and overall lesson success. Key words are 'participation', 'responsiveness', 'involved' and 'enjoyment'. Indeed, enjoyment was a word that cropped up many times in what teachers said to us in response to our question about the constituents of a specially good lesson. Cooper and McIntyre (1995) also found that a lesson was seen to have gone well when pupils appeared to show that they had enjoyed the lesson or appeared to have worked harmoniously together.

The criterion of pupil engagement with the task was also an important feature. 'All involved', 'maximum participation', 'task-orientated', the terms which appear in the citations, are characteristic of most in this category. Again, we recognize that this is an important element in the way that teachers evaluate their lessons, and it is reasonable to argue that the level of involvement can be subsequently considered against the products of pupils' work: essays, mathematical examples and other 'hard' evidence. Interestingly, the teachers in their explanations of 'successful' lessons do not connect these observed pupil behaviours either with product or with any particular methods and activities they deployed in the successful lesson. What does come through clearly as a signal of lesson success is that pupils are seen to be busy and enjoying what they are doing.

Sharp and Green (1975) have analysed and described (albeit for the primary school) pupils' levels of participation and involvement under the umbrella term *busyness*. To Sharp and Green, 'busyness' was a signal that all was well for the time being with pupils. With our teacher interviewees in the secondary school context, 'busyness' in terms of engagement was coupled with observed pupil enjoyment and teachers experiencing feelings of good relationships with pupils. It seemed clear from the nature of their comments that teachers were judging pupils' responses in this category largely by their body language.

Pleasure in pupils' expressions, often conveyed by the remark 'the light in the eyes of the pupils', has tended to be lampooned as a criterion, yet it does seem to constitute one important non-verbal signal of successful teaching. Body language, in all its forms, is an important means of human communication, and a question can be raised about the extent to which teachers have been formally trained to read the body language of pupils.

In addition to the various aspects of pupils' 'engagement' within this first sub-category of response, teachers gave their perceptions of the quality of interaction between themselves and pupils as another affective signal of the successful lesson. For example:

> There was empathy from the sixth form – we were on a social level. (M/11–20/HOD)

> When they treat me like part of a working team. (M/11–20/HOD)

> The chemistry of human interaction. (M/20+/HOD)

> Personal relationships are important – that they see me as a person. (F/11–20/HOY)

We have, in describing our research findings so far, noted that teachers in their response patterns tend to give a lowish ranking to the aspect of 'teacher–pupil' relationships in their work. Here teachers are endorsing their importance in relation to successful lessons, but what is interesting about the above comments, is the implication that they 'just happen'. They seem to convey passivity on the part of the teacher about good relationship – that somehow whether the relationship works to bring about a successful lesson is more the responsibility of the pupil.

Finally, within the 'affective' subcategory of responses about the constituents of successful lessons, there were a small number of comments referring mainly to pupils being motivated, or their self-belief being heightened, e.g.:

> It was a project lesson and there was a high level of participation and responsiveness to what I was doing. I was trying to give them self belief so that their confidence in tackling the project was raised. (M/1–10/CT).

Pupil response and instrumental factors

In this category we describe the 'instrumental' signals of successful lessons observed by teachers. The clear majority of responses in this subcategory (about 47 per cent of the total) referred to 'learning having taken place':

> When you have almost seen them thinking – after being given a different theory they answer the questions well. (M/20+/HOD)

> When the less able can write a few sentences. (F/11–20/HOY)

> When it is clear to me that they have understood what I have been aiming at. (F/1–10/CT)

It was a low ability group doing the life cycle of the honey bee. They connected the practical work with the relevant concepts. (M/20+/HOY)

Other reasons for successful lessons which we have labelled 'instrumental' were to do with objectives having been achieved (21 per cent):

They had achieved what I had set out to do. (F/20+/HOD)

Pupils achieving the objective and finishing the lesson with questioning. (F/1–10/CT)

A lesson about Macbeth. They caught on to what I wanted them to do. (F/1–10/CT)

The oral and written response from the children showed that I had achieved my objective. (M/11–20/CT)

Teachers also observed that pupils had been extended in the successful lessons:

When the work is challenging but enjoyable to the pupils. (M/1–10/CT)

Getting the most from yourself and the class – when pushed to the limit – drawing that bit extra out. (F/11–20/HOD)

There were four well chosen activities which meant high expectations of the pupils. (M/1–10/CT)

Finally in this 'instrumental' subcategory, the remaining comments (about 16 per cent of the total) referred to individuals as indicators of successful lessons:

Seeing a student take off – twisting your ideas and throwing them back at you. (M/20+/HOD)

When a girl who had been bottom of the heap starts participating. (F/20+/HOD)

In a Year 12 resit class a child suddenly became aware that something was for them – the pupil realized . . . potential. (F/20+/CT)

When a child succeeds and masters a given task, understanding the particular concept or idea. (M/11–20/HOD)

We were using artefacts – a Sikh bangle. One boy said: 'It's God – it has no beginning nor end'. (F/11–20/HOD)

Teachers denote successful lessons by signals they take from pupils' 'affective' or 'technical' responses. While teachers seem to connect the 'instrumental' successes with their own planning, presentation and activities generally, in their comments about the 'affective' or relationship aspects connected with successful lessons they seemed more ambiguous about their own role. We would, though, judge pupils' positive affective responses as an implied measure of teachers' appropriate use of effective learning activities and explanation.

Successful lessons: my methods of teaching

Responses which included a teacher factor, it will be recalled from Table 6.3, account for 35 per cent (just over one-third) of all factors we derived from their replies to the question. This can, as before, be subdivided, and we have constructed Table 6.5, which shows the frequency with which teachers link the elements connected with their own role with successful lessons.

As Table 6.5 shows, the responses in this subcategory were fairly wide-ranging, and among the seven shown there was no one really dominant element. The overwhelming majority of reasons were, however, connected with the *teaching processes* of planning, delivery and control. While there was an *affective* category, it related largely to comments about the teachers' own enthusiasm, and did not include any reference on her or his part to do with actions relating to pupil relationships and successful lessons.

The most frequent element in this subcategory is that which might be expected as a precondition for success, planning the lesson:

One that is organized and planned. (F/1–10/CT)

Well planned – you have to know what you are doing. (F/20+/CT)

Good preparation – I knew what I was talking about and was able to put it across in an enjoyable manner. (M/1–10/CT)

For the most part, but not entirely, the responses which we categorized under 'delivery' pointed up the need for a variety of learning activities to be presented to pupils. In this respect, teachers' definition of what constitutes success in a lesson matches an important component of pupils' definition of good teaching:

Table 6.5 Successful lessons: to do with 'my' methods of teaching (*n* = 86)

Subcategory	%
To do with planning of the lesson	13
To do with delivery of the lesson	9
To do with pitch of the lesson at right level	4.5
Teachers' enthusiasm/feelings	4.5
Lesson had been successfully given before	2
There was good class control	1
Resources used sparked a good response	1
Total %	35

It was a sixth form discussion and I played devil's advocate to challenge them to express their opinions. (F/1–10/CT)

A training session with year 11 – I used a teaching style that I had well established. (M/20+/HOY)

When I introduced a new topic. Used OHP and flash cards – you have to provide a natural setting for learning a language. (F/11–20/SM)

You need lots of different activities. (F/1–10/HOD)

Variety in tasks. (F/1–10/CT)

The delivery – it is important to break up the activities. (M/11–20/SM)

In general using a variety of methods such as role play. (M/20+/HOD)

And the careful time management of the lesson. (F/11–20/HOD)

Pitching work at a level appropriate to that of the pupil is related to both the planning and the delivery of a successful lesson, and is an important 'quality' element in teaching and learning, which pupils also pointed up:

Right level for the group – not too easy nor too difficult. (F/20+/SM)

Appropriate to the pupil's ability. (M/1–10/CT)

In a small number of cases, teachers attributed the success of the lesson to the fact that they had given it before and were repeating or building upon the experience:

Usually when I have tried the lesson before. (M/1–10/CT)

Aerial photography of children's own area – it works every year and leads on to 4/5 follow-up lessons. (M/1–10/CT)

In connecting successful lessons with their own actions, our teacher interviewees also made reference to their feelings, especially the degree of enthusiasm with which they conducted the lesson or lessons:

If I am enthusiastic, they will pick it up. (M/11–20/CT)

Where I am personally enthusiastic, I can spark off an interest, for example, in genetics. (M/1–10/SM)

Confidence in myself is a factor. (F/11–20/HOY)

The sun shines and the teacher is in a better mood. (F/11–20/CT)

There is nothing really surprising in the kind of reasons that teachers give in linking lesson success with their own classroom practices, for such aspects as lesson planning and delivery, which arouse interest by way of varied activities (as well as their own enthusiasm), are to be expected. What is to some extent surprising, however, is the relative absence of comments regarding control in the classroom or on issues to do with their management of pupil relationships.

Successful lessons: other factors

In Table 6.3 we indicated that about 14 per cent of all teachers' reasons for the specially good or successful lessons were connected with matters other than pupil responses or their own teaching methods. For the most part, these other reasons were connected with the subject content, without drawing out the way in which this feeds into the success of the lesson. For example:

> Pneumatics – teaching both bands in science. (M/1–10/CT)

However, seven teachers responded in a way which reflected the fact that the successful lesson could be the product of other, sometimes fortuitous, factors, even on occasions implying a *negation* of planning. For example:

> Their response is the most important factor rather than what you have prepared. (F/11–20/CT)

> It sometimes happens by accident – for example, the time of day affects the lesson. (F/11–20/SM)

> You can plan but it happens by chance. (F/1–10/CT)

> More opportunity than planning. (M/11–20/SM)

Teachers, teaching style and successful lessons: their perspectives on pedagogy

From the data which the teachers gave us in individual interviews in these comprehensive schools in response to our questions about their teaching style and constituents of their successful lessons, some broad conclusions emerge which raise issues about the whole status of pedagogy in school culture, professional discourse and training.

We would have to say that in our research experience as a whole we found the teachers, when invited to reveal their views on pedagogy, to be less like fountains gushing forth, and more like modest springs of information. In relation to styles of pedagogy, we found the majority of teachers did not take up the popular stereotypes of traditional and progressive teaching which were offered to them by the first of the two questions, although a significant number did describe themselves as *traditional*, with its connotation of largely expository style. The clear majority saw themselves as using a mixture of methods and strategies, but the description of these was far from detailed.

We were struck by the fact that, compared with their comments about pupils' learning, the teachers' responses did not suggest the same degree of readiness to engage with us on this topic. We inferred from this that, for them, explication of teaching styles was more of a challenge. More importantly, however, the analysis of their responses – the words and terms that they used and which we have tried to convey in the extracts – suggests not an absence of ideas about pedagogy but more a restricted code. In using this term we are borrowing from Bernstein's (1961) early and later formulations of the concept. The significant criterion of restricted codes is not so much that there is a reduction in the wealth of language but crucially that *meanings are shared, taken for granted and not made fully explicit.* In any culture there is an implied tendency for its members to share common facets of their life, so much so that it is not necessary always to make communications absolutely explicit.

We have remarked on the culture of the staffroom, which appeared to restrict the development and elaboration of considerations of pedagogy. In this respect, it was as if the interview room and teacher responses were an extension of the staff common room. Therefore, while across the range of teachers we interviewed, there were references to aspects of pedagogy, and collectively teachers do touch upon many important factors, on closer inspection, and at a more individual level, there was a tendency to leave potentially important lines of thought underdeveloped, and we failed to discern a clear common core across teachers' views on the classroom practices associated with teaching style.

Teachers' responses regarding 'successful' lessons were a little more detailed. Factors to do with their own teaching continued to take second place to teachers' emphasis upon the perceived responses by pupils, although we acknowledge that such pupil 'responses' can, at one extreme, be considered to be the result of teacher inputs. Nevertheless, the accounts given by teachers generally continued to imply a downplaying of their own role. We could hardly fail to notice that, by contrast with the way in which pupils elaborated their views on successful teaching, the teachers' contribution was of a more general nature.

Teachers also had less to say about their own work than they did about their pupils' responses. Moreover, when they elaborated upon their pedagogical stance, they focused mainly upon procedural/organizational and pupil-oriented factors in relation to pedagogy, and 'wrote themselves into the account' with only about one in five of all factors. Hence, if the teaching–learning process is taken to be essentially one of interaction between the two parties – a transactional process – what the teachers said reveals a significant asymmetry. Considering the nature of teachers' responses to our questions about pedagogy in the round, it seems evident to us that what they said reflected a work context and culture where they have little opportunity to discuss pedagogy in any systematic or generic way. Indeed, a range of writers have drawn attention to the constraints on the discussion of pedagogy within the culture of teaching within Britain generally.

There is, for example, the classic paper by Simon (1994): 'Why no pedagogy in England?' Simon wrote that:

> pedagogy itself implies structure. It implies the elaboration or definition of specific means adapted to produce the desired effect – such-and-such learning on the part of the child. From the start the use of the term, pedagogy has been concerned to relate the process of teaching to that of learning on the part of the child . . . For a combination of social, political, and ideological reasons pedagogy . . . has never taken root and flourished in Britain.
>
> (Simon 1994: 14–15)

We see the present day culture of schools as reflecting this inheritance. The restricted range of teachers' views about their classroom methods, which we collected and have illustrated, reflects the reality of the culture of schools, where there is generally a relative absence of discourse and discussion on pedagogy. Nor has this generic aspect of all teachers' work ever had, as far as we can see, any prominence in public policy for teachers' continuing professional development. What we found would still generally support what Hargeaves wrote, that there is:

> a culture of autonomous individualism which permeates the whole of the teaching profession, with competence being attributed only to those who demonstrate they can manage alone. Individualism, intuitive teacher knowledge and anxieties about competencies inhibit the emergence of co-operative solutions and a widely shared professional ideology. So what arises in their place are coping strategies, which then retreat into individualism. Teachers are therefore closed off from ideological consensus and the possibility of a genuinely integrated code, and their occupational culture is highly resistant to change.
>
> (Cited in Beynon 1985: 13)

There is, of course, a delicate balance between the pragmatic enacting of professional roles and their theoretical and conceptual bases, and we are by no means deprecating the former. Much of a teacher's work will be guided by experience and practice, building upon success and rejecting less successful practices, and we have already drawn attention to the achievements of secondary teachers in broadening the range of pupils who complete their course with significant achievements at GCSE. In the day-to-day hurly-burly of the classroom there is little time for leisurely reflection upon matters of pedagogy. And this is something which some schools have begun to recognize by programmes of staff training.

While we were completing this book, *The Times,* for example, was carrying a story about a Wiltshire school where since 1990 all staff have contributed to in-service training designed to improve classroom performance: 'at training meetings teachers described the teaching techniques which had worked well for them. The English department outlined how it ran group research and reported back as a classroom exercise. The Science department was fascinated and adapted it to fit its needs. The Humanities department described how it used role play. With their interest sparked, teachers then gave up free lessons to watch one another teach. Classroom groupings were analysed to find why troublesome pupils worked well in certain settings but not others.' Such comings together to exchange practice and ideas about pedagogy across the subject range on a generic basis are yet to become the rule rather than the exception.

Given the pressures of everyday school life and the lack of the sort of opportunities such as those in the school just referred to, when teachers are called to account, as it were, by the nature of questions such as those we put, is there justification in expecting a more measured and developed response than we received? This issue has received renewed consideration by some modern thinkers. Peter Jarvis (1997) distinguishes between non-reflective learning, which involves (*inter alia*) the learning of skills, and reflective learning, which includes contemplation, reflective skill and a willingness to experiment and be creative. Michael Eraut (1997) observed that research into how teachers and managers think and work concluded that good practitioners had an enormously complex and *highly personal* knowledge base, constructed from experience *but used in a fairly intuitive way*. Eraut develops his argument in a way that echoes Jarvis's levels of learning. He distinguishes between skilled behaviours – a routinized sequence of complex actions – and deliberative processes involving a complexity of different types of knowledge, all of which lie at the heart of professional work.

What Jackson and Eraut are arguing is that there are essentially two levels of professional knowledge which characterize teachers (and managers), of which the first is relevant here to what we have been calling technical skills, which are developed predominantly through the routine enactment of the tasks which fall to them. These are performed without much conscious thinking and become, as the teacher gains experience, routinized. Eraut sums up this state of professional knowledge as 'tacit knowledge, something which is not easily explained to others or even to oneself'. If he is correct in this observation, then the responses to our questions about pedagogy may well be characterized by tacit knowledge and the inability to explain.

The message from teachers in this chapter is that they define good teaching mainly from the response behaviours of pupils to their lessons and from judgements about their own planning and teaching methods, but in their comments they do not connect the two in a very explicit way.

Postscript: our research methods and teachers' pedagogy

We did not complete a systematic analysis of the teachers' data from the two questions we had posed, until we had nearly completed our interviewing in the schools. It was therefore late in the day when we came to appreciate the relative parsimony of pedagogical constructs from teachers in response to the two questions which had been specifically included for the purpose. Had we done so earlier, we would have added a more direct follow up question, something along the lines of 'Tell me in detail about the teaching methods and classroom strategies you adopt on a regular basis in your work', in order to receive teacher views not caught by the two questions we had used. We are sure that there is much more scope for further research which investigates what teachers do in the classroom and its connection with learning outcomes.

7 | Teachers' and pupils' perspectives compared: shared or dissimilar?

In Chapters 2–6 when discussing the responses from the two sets of participants to our questions, we occasionally made some reference to teachers when considering pupils' perspectives and vice versa, but we did not at the time draw out the similarities or differences in any overall, summative way. The purpose of this chapter is to do that, to draw together comparisons into a unified discussion.

In that respect, we do not here consider any new material, but present judgements from the research data we have discussed: whether the two groups (pupils' and teachers' comments) coincide, diverge or simply do not relate to each other regarding their perspectives on a given topic of teaching and learning. In undertaking this task, we to an extent inevitably revisit some of the data we have discussed. In Chapter 1, we described the basis upon which we intended to align the two sets of responses – those of teachers and of pupils – by putting questions to each group that would elicit data covering similar areas. By asking both groups about differences in rates of learning, we were able to demonstrate the factors that interviewees from both groups believed to be important. The question about a best lesson was intended to focus the two sets of respondents on issues of pedagogy. Other non-parallel issues to do with pedagogy were raised: pupils were asked about 'good teaching', and teachers about their style of teaching. The product regarding pedagogy therefore constituted a broad canvas, and we have had, of necessity, to extract some significant features of the landscape, acknowledging that others might go unstated. In the title of this chapter the question is asked whether the perspectives which emerged were shared or dissimilar. As might be expected, the outcomes were more complex than such a simple dichotomous categorization. We believe that a comparison of pupil and teacher perspectives reveals four categories of contrast (Table 7.1).

There are some perspectives which are shared in similar fashion by both teachers and pupils, and there are some which we have labelled 'disparate'. By this we mean that there are some perspectives which, though they

Table 7.1 Pupil and teacher views of learning and teaching: perspectives contrasted

Opposed perspectives	*Unilateral perspectives*	*Shared perspectives*	*Disparate perspectives*
About learning more or better	Importance of humour and having some fun (for pupils)	About the importance of pedagogy: teaching methods	Regarding the importance and focus of interpersonal relationship factors
		About the relative importance of the subject	Regarding the importance of classroom control and order
			Regarding priorities about teaching methods

are shared by both pupils and teachers to the extent that they use the same terms, the same explanatory or causal categories, they are not shared in the same way with each other. Pupils and teachers are disparate in that there are significant differences in the degree of influence which each ascribes to the category, and even differences in 'kind' regarding the constituents of the causal category.

We have categorized two other types of perspective comparisons: what we have called 'opposed perspectives', where the views of one group exhibit the almost opposite profile to that of the other; and 'unilateral perspectives', where, as the name implies, the perspective has been exhibited by only one of the two respondent groups in answers to our questions. Table 7.1 displays these four categories, and we discuss them in the order in which they are set out.

Opposed perspectives

We see only one topic area to do with teaching and learning, on which the perspectives of the participants are wholly opposed, and that is to do with the ability of pupils to 'learn more' or 'learn better' (Table 7.2). As we demonstrated in Chapters 2 and 5, both teachers and pupils used similar attribution categories in responding to their respective questions about learning. When the percentage responses which the two groups gave to these categories are set alongside each other as we have done in Table 7.2, while some remarkable similarities are exhibited for some subcategories, on the core issue of differential learning, teachers believe that this is overwhelmingly to do with the pupils themselves, substantially with their endowed ability and home background. Pupils in directly opposite response believe that their differential learning is overwhelmingly to do with the behaviour of teachers, principally with their teaching methods and

Table 7.2 Learning 'more/better': pupil and teacher percentage responses compared by category

Category	All pupils	All teachers
To do with the teacher	60	18
To do with the pupil	23	62
To do with the subject	7	9
Miscellaneous reasons	10	11
Totals	100	100

social relationships in the classroom. There is, therefore, a reversal of the prioritizing of the roles for the two parties engaged in the process of learning. Moreover, as we showed, these opposed perspectives were consistent for both groups across all the schools irrespective of location, size or character of the school.

Both teachers and pupils place the other's role centre stage in the learning process. For the teachers, however, their construction of child-centredness brings with it the dangers of adopting something of a deterministic and fatalistic position. 'If they haven't got the requisite number of IQ points and are not from homes with a supportive ethos then the chances for the children are not good' is a crude but by no means inaccurate summation of their stance. The pupils' response to the teachers' position seems to be along the lines of: 'It is not where we are, in our grasp of the curriculum, but where we can be, with your help.' The teacher for them is the significant agent, and they can offer a wealth of detail about what teacher and teaching qualities, in their opinion, bring about effective learning.

Unilateral perspectives

The importance of humour and having some fun was, as we showed earlier, a consistent requirement for pupils. They want teachers to lubricate day-to-day work with the oil of humour. Humour could be linked in their comments with all aspects of teachers' classroom work, with aspects of teaching methods, relationships or with the keeping of control in the classroom:

It's good if the teacher keeps it interesting with humour. (G-M-9)

I like it when they have a joke and make you do the work. (G-U-7)

Some teachers are more friendly, will have a laugh and listen more. (B-M-8)

Some teachers don't have a laugh and a joke. (B-L-9)

Some explain things better than others, you can have a bit of a laugh with them. (B-M-10)

Strict enough to make us learn, yet have a laugh. (G-U-9)

While pupils referred to the place and importance of humour and asserted that good teaching is socially pleasant and work-directed, no teacher in discussing his or her style of teaching or successful lessons made any mention at all of humour, or of creating or having had some fun. It was clear from the whole demeanour of pupils in commenting about humour that teachers who have the skill of imparting some humour while maintaining a strong sense of direction and work engagement are very highly rated, and we formed the clear impression that those who are best at imparting humour have definite acting skills, both verbally and non-verbally.

Humour or having a bit of fun in the classroom was something commented about only by pupils, then, although it was inevitable that some of the teachers we spoke to must have been seen by their pupils as possessing 'humour and fun' skills. With one science teacher whom several interviewees in one school gave as an exemplar of good teaching methods, his graphic and humorous acting methods were commented on, but when he was interviewed the following day we received no comment on this aspect of his approach at all. We wonder whether this is because professional tradition has it that teaching should not be seen (or confessed to) as a performing art, as some have argued (Rives 1979). Rives has argued that, like performing artists, teachers have an audience to engage, a stage or place to perform, something to communicate, modes and style of performance, in that they can operate in both solo or ensemble mode, and an instrument to 'play', i.e. themselves. Hence, as performing artists, at least to some extent, teachers should learn everyday theatrical skills: how to use certain body actions, facial and voice modulation to convey emotions, mind sets and subtle messages etc. This view does not require all teachers to become Laurence Oliviers, but it does suggest that teachers who learn some actors' performance skills will be better teachers. We are convinced that some training in these skills would equip teachers better to enact the challenging balance between the detailed affective and technical skills which their pupils associate with effective learning and good teaching.

Shared perspectives

We see there to be two perspectives which are shared by pupils and teachers to some significant extent. These are to do with the role of classroom teaching methods and of the subject in effective learning and good teaching.

Table 7.3 Importance of methods to teachers and pupils

Teachers	% response	Pupils	% response
Importance by % weight of comment on methods in discussing style of teaching	62	Importance by % weight of comment in 'learning more' – to do with the teacher	60
Importance by % weight of comment in discussing successful lessons	35	Importance by % weight of comment on 'better teachers' – good classroom practices	46

Teachers, pupils and pedagogy

The two parties give comparable levels of importance to the place of pedagogy in their definitions of good teaching and successful lessons. We indicate this in Table 7.3 by contrasting some measures we have already displayed in earlier tables, which conveyed analyses of answers to questions by both parties. In comparing the place of pedagogy, we are here referring essentially to the teachers' methods of presentation and explanation of subject material and the learning activities associated with the topic, rather than the aspect of classroom control and order, or teacher–pupil relationships, for which we make comparisons later in this chapter. As Table 7.3 shows, 62 per cent of teachers' answers about style of teaching concerned teaching methods, while 60 per cent of all pupils' comments about 'learning more' were connected with some aspect of teaching methods. The parties also gave a comparable weight of comment about teaching methods in response to other questions, as Table 7.3 also shows.

The parties share a common perspective of the importance of teachers' classroom methods, then, and it might be observed that there is nothing very surprising in this, that it self-evidentially would be the case. However, is the importance they attach to teaching methods of the same nature for both parties, or are there differences to the detail? It is clear from the evidence we received that there are disparities of view regarding the *value* accorded to the role of 'methods', to what we are calling the desired *methods framework*, and in respect of an assumed relationship between appropriate methods and the ability group of pupils. We discuss these below, along with the other items in the 'disparate perspectives' category.

Teachers, pupils and the subject

Table 7.2 reminds us that pupils and teachers have similar perspectives regarding the role of the subject in learning 'more' or 'better'. Indeed, in the responses to our enquiries on all the other aspects of good teaching and learning, we consistently saw the role of the individual subject to be minimal.

In Chapter 3, where we described the pupil view of the differences between 'good' and 'less good' teaching, the subject aspect of teachers' classroom work was also of little significance. In Chapter 5, the teachers saw pupils' attachment to a particular subject to be the least significant among the categories of reasons accounting for pupils learning at different rates. Moreover, in Chapter 6, we found that teachers gave subject aspects a low status in explanation of the constituents of *the successful lesson*. In some ways we are somewhat surprised by the weight given to the position of the subject by both pupils and teachers.

In our research work connected with the TVEI implementation in the 1980s, which, of course, covered subjects in general and not just those directly concerned with the technical and vocational, we learned that, for pupils, subject choice and liking appeared to be of great importance, so we would have expected pupil weightings to be higher. It could be that, with the drastic restriction of pupil choice consequent on the establishment of the National Curriculum, the specific subject has much less salience. In the case of teachers, it was often widely held that their professional persona is compounded not only of technical or 'professional' expertise, but also of subject expertise. One is not so much a teacher but a *science* teacher, for example, and teachers are always asked *what* do you teach, and not *how* do you teach? We had therefore expected to receive more comments invoking links with subject matter in the answers to our questions about learning and teaching. The fact that we did not, from either pupils or teachers, means that the conclusion from all of this is inescapable: the components of *quality* in teaching and learning are generic; they cross all subject boundaries and apply to all classrooms; and this is a matter where the perspectives of pupils and teachers are shared and agree with each other.

Disparate perspectives

Just as our category of shared perspectives meant that the perspectives were significantly similar to each other but not entirely the same, those we have labelled 'disparate' are perspectives which are significantly dissimilar between teachers and pupils, but not entirely different. There were three examples of disparate perspectives, and the first of these concerns teacher–pupil relationships, for which we see there to be differences in both kind and degree.

The importance of interpersonal relationships

We have seen in earlier chapters how good relationships provide for pupils an important context for their work in the classroom. Their main

Table 7.4 Importance of teacher–pupil (T–P) relationships: pupil and teacher perspectives contrasted

Pupils	% response	Teachers	% response
Importance by weight of comment on T–P relationships within all reasons for why learning more	10.25	Importance by weight of comment on T–P relationships within all reasons for why pupils learn better	5
Importance by weight of comment on T–P relationships within all reasons for why some teachers teach better	28.6	Importance by weight of comment on T–P relationships within all comments on approaches to teaching	6

concerns are that teachers: are friendly people; are a constant source of help to their problems of learning; treat them with respect as individuals; and do not raise the noise level or cause fear by shouting at them.

Consequently, the concern of pupils for effective teacher relationships was reflected in the indicative measures we obtained in the answers to our questions about 'learning more' and 'good teaching'. As well as the very consistent set of constructs regarding relationships expressed by pupils in all schools, a significant weight of comment was given to this aspect of teacher behaviour, as we show in the summary positions conveyed by Table 7.4. In their ranking of the factors to do with learning more, pupils ranked relationships in fourth position out of eight categories of reasons, and in their ranking of the factors which characterize 'good teaching' and 'good teachers', the teacher's interpersonal style and relations was ranked first out of seven categories. Teacher–pupil relationships therefore have a prime position in the pupils' perspective of what counts as effective teaching and learning, but this degree of importance is not the same for teachers.

As Table 7.4 shows, while teacher–pupil relationships were not ignored by teachers, this factor carries significantly less weight with them, and they accorded it a much lower degree of importance within the totality of reasons they gave in response to our questions about pupil learning and successful lessons. As we have suggested, it is very clear that teachers and pupils accord a very different level of importance to the aspect of teacher–pupil relationships. However, the evidence also suggests that the difference is not just one of degree, but one in kind.

When pupils replied to our questions, almost always they were thinking in a self-centred way about relationships, and we are using the term in a non-pejorative sense here. They were crucially concerned with themselves as individual learners and with their own performance and success in the process, however this is measured. Although not ignoring relationships with the class in general, their standpoint, in short, was heavily concerned with the *personal relationship* between them as individuals and their teachers, as the examples we gave in Chapter 3 testify.

Teachers, on the other hand, confront classes and groups of pupils. That is their professional reality, and it will be recalled that group work featured strongly in explaining their overall orientation to teaching. But only a handful of them saw *success on the part of an individual pupil* as an important factor. In managing relationships with learners, *a priori* teachers have to operate at two levels so that they positively enhance pupil identity as a member of the group and also as an individual. From the first can come the notion of ordinary people collectively achieving extraordinary standards, and from the second the nurturing and development of individuals. No easy task!

The focus of teachers' replies in respect of relationships was different from that of the pupils. Whereas pupils focused on, as we have said, their own personal relationship with the teacher almost as a strategic proactive factor in their own learning, the core focus of teachers' comments was different. Teachers focused on good class relationships, more as something to do with the social climate of the classroom in general than as an issue of maintaining dyadic relationships with pupils. In this respect, teacher–pupil relationships were for teachers more a matter of context and more to be taken for granted. Indeed, while there was some acknowledgement of their own responsibility, there seemed also to be some hesitancy *vis-à-vis* their own role in creating positive relationships, and some suggested that the quality of relationships can lie beyond their control, perhaps even in the lap of the gods.

We are not suggesting that these disparate views of relationships mean that this element is of no professional concern to teachers, but that it is currently both a more 'taken for granted' factor in their professional work and restricted in focus in comparison with the pupils' view of the connection between relationships and effective learning and teaching. We see the implication of this as the need for the creation of relationships appropriate to effective classroom teaching to be recognized as a desirable teacher skill, and not left to the whims of personality or other chance circumstances. Pupils have given clear leads about the content of relationships skills training.

Classroom control and order

It will be recalled that 'control and order' was decidedly important to pupils. This factor accounted for nearly 14 per cent of all reasons and occupied second ranking among the eight categories given by pupils for them learning more in some lessons than others. Control and order also constituted about 11 per cent of all reasons and was ranked fourth among the seven categories given by pupils to explain why some teachers teach better than others. In the forced choice written exercise – 'the lessons where I learn most' – the 'control and order' item, 'There is not too much mucking about', was ranked second out of the eleven items.

Order in the classroom was therefore a definite requirement of pupils, but we stress again that these numerical measures are meant to be indicative. The same number of statements can be made for two different sets of factors. Yet in the case of one set, the statements might have been made with a force and emphasis lacking for the second category. This, as we said earlier, was often true for the statements on 'control and order' made by pupils; they were often given great emphasis, as well as being made disproportionately by those designated lower ability pupils.

For teachers there was a disparate position. While they did not leave 'control and order' out of account in their general approaches to teaching, or within the reasons attributed to their successful lesson (2.3 per cent of total reasons), its degree of importance was never as prominent for them as it was for pupils. Nor were teachers' 'control and order' comments connected with learning outcomes as frequently as were those of the pupils. There was a tendency for them to see this aspect of classroom practice linked more to their own authority or power position. Qualitatively, we were clear that there was a disparity between the two perspectives. Pupils want to experience more order and control, and they appear to be more aware of its importance to learning than was expressed in the teachers' comments.

Priorities about teaching methods

The evidence we received shows that while their relative importance is shared, there are some differences between teachers and pupils regarding the *value* they accorded to the role of 'methods' in learning, the desired *methods ownership framework*, and methods and *type of child*.

Pupils place very great value on the relationship between a teacher's methods and the achievement of learning, whereas for teachers this link was weaker in the comments made. In Chapter 6, for example, in accounting for their successful lessons (Table 6.3), we saw that 'my teaching methods', were not given the predominant status which might reasonably have been assumed, and we see this as reflecting teachers' beliefs regarding the extent to which they can affect pupils' learning when set against the odds of pupils' innate endowments and home background, which we evidenced in Chapter 5.

It also seems to be the case that pupils and teachers have differing emphases regarding the *ownership framework* and classroom teaching methods. Here the distinction we shall make is based on the notion that *ownership of learning* implies a transactive view, so that pupils and teachers are joint owners. They are placed together within a context of mutual exchange, so that both have need of the other and both are able to offer the other the potential, jointly, to maximize learning effectiveness. But the relationship is transactional with an important rider attached. The power relationship between the two parties is not symmetrical – teachers' status requires them to take a lead in constructing the reality of the classroom. This does not, of course, rule out the establishment of a *methods framework* where the potential for pupil involvement is maximized. Teachers can set a framework where the relationships between the two are strongly bounded or otherwise.

The so-called traditional and progressive modes of teaching, which formed the basis of a question about how teachers describe their general approach to teaching, imply issues of strong and weak framing. The first of these lies at the heart of 'chalk and talk' approaches, which character-ized to a greater or lesser extent the nearly 40 per cent of teachers whose responses fitted the traditional or tending towards the traditional. We can recall the teacher who could not afford to allow pupils to discover things for themselves, because, it was argued, they might discover 'untrue' things. Here, not only is the subject matter strongly bounded by the teacher, but the process of teaching set up to ensure that the 'true path' is followed implies strongly differentiated relationships between the two sets of actors. There is, in short, a clear-cut role for the teacher and one for the learner.

Although she did not elaborate in detail, another teacher who stated that she was 'non-traditional in that I involve the pupils, I pass the respons-ibility to them', illustrates a markedly different position and one that potentially allows for the weakening of traditional roles between teachers and taught and thereby the empowerment of pupils in the framing of teaching methods. Examples of this position, needless to say, are less fre-quently represented on our scale, and such a pedagogical stance carries with it greater challenges and risks to both groups compared with the tra-ditional style. We are therefore suggesting a distinction between a bounded framework and a transactive framework to teaching methods, to reflect the relative distinction in methods priorities which teachers and pupils expressed to us.

From the comments which we amply illustrated in Chapters 3 and 4, comprehensive school pupils have clearly defined and convergent views about pedagogy, have a very common vocabulary and are clear about what for them is effective teaching. We see their priorities as making complex demands upon teachers. They not only demand sympathetic, extensive and effective explanation on the part of the teacher, but also want, at the same time, the opportunity to find out things for themselves by way of imaginative activities. They seemed clearly to be asking for more loosen-ing of the delivery of the curriculum – a less bounded and more *transactive* framework. They are demanding the inclusion of the teacher in the trans-action, of course, but that involvement needs to be measured and well directed, not all-encompassing and stifling of pupils' active involvement.

Pupils of all ability groups across all schools clearly favoured the use of a variety of teaching methods and a limited use of traditional or exposit-ory methods. There were no traditionalists among them, for we encoun-tered no single pupil whose views amounted to a plea for traditional teaching as it is defined both popularly and by the teachers themselves. There was no counterpart among pupils of the 20 per cent of teachers who defined themselves as 'traditional', and whose views we illustrated in Chapter 6.

A significant proportion of teachers we interviewed also believed there to be a relationship between the type of teaching methods which should be used and the ability group of the pupils being taught. This view is not shared by their pupils. We have examined the data carefully, and there is no disposition expressed by designated upper ability pupils for more formal methods, nor any indication that they prefer teaching methods which are different in any way from those favoured by all other pupils. Pupils of all abilities have the same definitions of good teaching.

Shared and contrasting perspectives: the implications

There appear to be two broad implications from the shared and contrasting perspectives we have discussed. First, in respect of the relative responsibilities for learning taken by the two key participants in teaching and learning, there is a patent need to address the opposed perspectives currently existing between pupils and teachers. The evidence was clear-cut that at the present time both teachers and pupils apportion too much responsibility to the other party. Teachers are in need of greater belief that their teaching can make a bigger difference to pupils' learning than they currently think. While the creation of learning experiences will always be the teacher's prime responsibility, pupils do not currently express a sense that they have an ownership role in their own learning, or refer to any explicit pupil 'ownership activities' to do with their learning.

Second, and arising from shared perspectives regarding the importance of teaching methods, as well as from the disparate perspectives about the other aspects of classroom practice ('relationships', 'control and order' and priorities regarding teaching methods), there is a need for much more sharing of issues to do with pedagogy. While there is every reason for teachers to engage in discussion with pupils about pedagogy, principally the discussion needs to be between teachers and teachers, informed, of course, by what is known to be the rich pedagogic need expressed by the pupil perspective. As the new century approaches, teachers are working in the most demanding of environments. Their pupils can be saturated by the stimuli and excitement of all that comes from television, video, interactive arcade games and other information technology facilities which now invade the home. Against all this, teachers must compete, and the question that arises from all of this is: what repertoire of generic skills and methods is needed by teachers in secondary comprehensive schools for the twenty-first century?

We certainly do not have a ready answer, but were we to face the awesome challenge of a secondary school teacher's current situation, we would want to be equipped with as great a repertoire of methods, learning activities and relationship skills as possible. We would expect government and our employers to arrange the opportunities for us to update ourselves on these, and, moreover, to have some conception of what quantity of time is needed within our working contracts for adequately preparing demanding learning materials and activities, and for renewing these on an ongoing basis.

We realize that from a basis of presenting and discussing comparisons of pupil and teacher perspectives to do with learning and teaching, we have taken it on ourselves to make some strong prescriptive claims regarding what ought to be some policy responses to the picture we have described. We have been moved to do so because at the time of completing this book there is much discussion in the media regarding the progress (or lack of it) made in schools, the numbers of unsatisfactory lessons given 'last year' and the number of bad teachers in the system. But we have heard nothing about what needs to be done for teachers to enable them to improve further the quality of teaching and learning.

8 | Pupil and teacher perspectives on learning and teaching quality: issues for policy-makers

In the previous chapters we have presented and discussed findings on pupil and teacher perspectives from research to do with the quality of learning and teaching we carried out in ten comprehensive schools over a five-year period between 1992 and September 1997. We think that what these pupils and teachers revealed in their answers is a resource which can contribute to secondary schools becoming more effective. While the teachers and pupils are the principal 'owners' of what happens in the classroom, there are the other key stakeholders in what the classrooms of the comprehensive schools achieve. There is the wider community by way of 'government', as well as each individual school's own leadership and management, who determine many of the rules for, and resource, the classroom context in which teachers and pupils transact.

By government, we are essentially referring to the national framework of policy and rules for statutory education and the employment of teachers led and set in England by the Department for Education and Employment (DfEE) and its related agencies, such as the Teacher Training Agency and the Qualifications and Curriculum Authority, and, of course, their parallel or devolved counterparts in Scotland and Wales. We are suggesting, therefore, that what the pupils and teachers have had to say on the topics we discussed in the previous chapters has implications both for government policy and for each other.

Similarly, the classroom context in which teachers and pupils work together is shaped not only from 'outside and above', as it were, by government, but also from 'within and above' by the head and senior management team, who, together with the governing body, are charged with managing the effectiveness of the individual school. What the pupils and teachers said about learning and teaching also has implications for these school managers, and we shall consider below what these might be.

In this concluding chapter, then, we are attempting to tease out from our research findings what the implications are for policy and action in the whole context of effective teaching and learning by these four sets of stakeholders: government, school managers, teachers and the pupils themselves. Prior to considering the issues for each of these parties in turn, it is relevant to consider the applicability of the research findings we have described to comprehensive schooling in Britain generally.

The research findings and their applicability to other schools

An important key issue which arises for all educational research is the extent to which its conclusions can be reasonably held to have relevance and apply to other schools of the same type, and this is referred to in research methodology discussion as the issue of empirical generalization. We believe that the findings presented in this book can be generalized to other British comprehensive schools and are of relevance to secondary schooling generally, for two sets of reasons. First, the perspectives recorded were remarkably consistent across ten socially and demographically very different schools. Even the polar cases among them, the most 'affluent/ league table successful' school, and the most 'deprived/modest performance' school, had a similar profile and weighting of responses in the answers to the same key questions from both pupils and teachers, indicating, we would claim, that the research questions were tapping perspectives generic to all cases or schools of this type.

We know that similar social and demographic profiles to these ten schools can be found everywhere in Britain, which is also the case with regard to their academic performance levels. Taking as an index of performance the percentage of pupils who achieved five or more good grade GCSEs in 1997, the performance range of our ten schools (Table 8.1) represents the same sort of spread which exists for comprehensive schools in, for example, Somerset, Durham, Essex, Cheshire or other parts of Britain, as well as in Wales.

In Chapter 1, we indicated that we asked each of the research schools to provide us, within the sample profile we had requested, with a similar proportion of pupils receiving free school meals as existed in their school's

Table 8.1 Academic achievement in the ten schools: percentage of pupils achieving five GCSEs, grades A–C

Pupils achieving five GCSEs, grades A–C	*Schools in category*	*% of schools in category*
< 30%	H, I	20
30–59%	A, B, C, F, G, J	60
≥ 60%	D, E	20

Table 8.2 Free school meal pupils in the ten schools

Free school meal category	% of schools in category
Low (< 20% of pupils)	40
Middle (21–39% of pupils)	40
High (≥ 40% of pupils)	20

population as a whole, and this they did. It is widely held that this indicator is a good proxy for a range of social diversity which exists in pupils' home backgrounds and lives generally, and if used along with the representative proportions for gender, ability group and year group factors, creates a sound stratified sampling basis for interviewing. The proportion of pupils receiving free school meals varied among the ten schools from a low of 12 per cent to a high of 53 per cent, with a mean of 27 per cent (Table 8.2).

These ten schools reflected the ranges of both social and academic attainment, and appear to us to be representative of the diversity of comprehensive schools across the UK. The perspectives we recorded in these ten schools were consistent among pupils irrespective of age, gender or ability designation, and, in the case of teachers, of gender, subject taught or length of service. Given that the perspectives we recorded were also consistent irrespective of a school's size, social profile or academic attainment, we feel confident that the findings can be generalized to other secondary comprehensive schools.

Second, the findings of pupil and teacher perspectives on aspects of classroom learning and teaching, which we have presented in the earlier chapters, replicate and substantially extend, rather than conflict with, what previous British research invoking pupil views has found from other schools. We particularly have in mind here the research embracing pupil perspectives by Nash (1973), Woods (1979), Beynon (1985), Lang (1993) and Rudduck (1996), which has provided some data on teaching and learning issues and which derived from schools in quite different parts of the UK from ours. Their findings coincide almost entirely with those presented here, so that the views we have recorded from Wales parallel what has been found to be the case in different areas of England and Scotland. Moreover, our findings are also wholly congruent with parallel studies which have been carried out in North America such as the work by Mishra (1980) and Phelan *et al.* (1992). It would seem, therefore, that there are strong grounds for concluding that many of the detailed teaching–learning requirements which we have described in respect of the pupils in these ten British schools represent the generic requirements of students in these age groups, wherever they are in 'Western culture'.

For the above reasons, we see the evidence we have presented as raising valid issues for all comprehensive schools. We see our own contribution to this topic area as having produced research evidence which is focused on the perspectives of the main actors in the classroom; which gives clear empirical evidence of the detailed component categories of good learning, and of their relative weight or importance to pupils and teachers.

Issues for government

Government has since the 1980s been concerned with the effectiveness of schools, and it has in its policies taken on board many of the messages from the range of researches on school effectiveness (Reynolds 1985). In general, while the desiderata for teaching and learning quality set out by government via its various agencies appear to us to be largely clear, we think that there are questions arising from our research findings as to whether they embrace all the issues. Moreover, there does not seem to be a recognition of the nature of the resources needed for achievement of the 'quality' objectives.

For government and educational policy, we see the issues raised from the research we have reported to fall in the following areas: teacher training; teacher performance standards and the criteria of schools' inspection; the scope of the standard contract of work for teachers; policy for the in-service education and training provision for teachers; and government's setting of the appropriate rhetoric and climate for schools achievement generally.

Over recent years the standards which must be met in teacher training to achieve qualified teacher status (QTS), or to be demonstrated in a teacher's daily classroom performance and revealed for public scrutiny by external inspection, have been set down: first, by the Department for Education (DfE), and subsequently by the government agency of the Teacher Training Agency (TTA) and Ofsted (the Office for Standards in Education or OHMCI in Wales), respectively. These sources have indicated in some detail the competences required, and training institutions such as our own university have made explicit their own requirements for the 'teaching competences and professional qualities' which must be demonstrated in order to achieve QTS, for example.

To what extent, then, do the pupil and teacher perspectives of the research described in this book reveal matters not at present caught, or not as fully expressed in such documents, whether they are to do with teacher training or the inspection of what is happening in secondary school classrooms?

In 1997, the TTA in its document 'Standards for the award of qualified teacher status' said it was replacing the more general competences set out in a range of DfE circulars from 1992 with a detailed specification of standards for QTS, and we have compared our research findings with these standards. TTA standards set out a good deal about the knowledge, teaching and class management requirements which teachers must reach in order to qualify and subsequently demonstrate in their work. When these are compared with what our pupils said they wanted in good teachers, a great deal of what they said matches the TTA requirements. However, there is an absence in the TTA document of any detailed specifications regarding the teacher–pupil relationship behaviours expected, or the standards which need be demonstrated in respect of classroom control and order, two very important quality categories in the pupils' eyes across all schools. What the TTA document says about teaching methods *per se* matches closely the detail of the pupil perspective we described, save for the fact that, although 'explanation' is mentioned, the properties of what should constitute acceptable standards of explanation are not spelled out, something our pupil respondents did in some detail.

Similarly, we have matched the research findings with the content of Ofsted documents and found that, while the criteria of good teaching and learning practice they specify are comprehensive, they do not convey the sort of detail to do with the required teacher–pupil relations or the other aspects of classroom practice which the pupil perspective so clearly spelled out. In fact they are generally 'stated' at too high a level of abstraction compared with the day-to-day detail which concerns the pupil. In the light of the pupil perception evidence, then, Ofsted needs to consider for its teacher training and performance standards the writing-in, or the more prominent 'writing-up', of the skill categories to do with teacher–pupil relations and the enactment of control and order in the classroom.

A further issue concerns what pupils want in terms of classroom practice. As we described in Chapters 3 and 4, pupils want less expository teaching, more activity/practical based learning and more interpersonal attention, help, explanation, control and order from teachers. This is the very pedagogic area that coincides with sections in the 1997 TTA Standards document under the heading of 'B, Planning, teaching and class management', which covers:

> setting tasks for whole class, individual and group work, including homework, which challenges pupils and ensure high levels of pupil interest [. . . also]

> ensure effective teaching of whole classes, and of groups and individuals within the whole class setting.

What the TTA and comprehensive school pupils want therefore largely coincide, but what are the implications for already busy teachers? It seems self-evident to us that what the pupils and the TTA want for a best quality classroom practice demands considerable teacher preparation time in order to deliver more practical and activity-based teaching and learning, and therein lies a problem. The vast majority of the teachers we interviewed taught a full timetable. They also had significant administrative record keeping to do alongside their class teaching. Given the fact that the total hours in a week are immutable and that teachers like everyone else have domestic lives, we do not see where the required preparation time can come from within current contractual conditions, if teachers are to refine and update their classroom methods, materials and activities in response to needs arising during the working term.

Another issue for government which arises from both the teacher and pupil perspectives on pedagogy is the need for a more open discussion of pedagogy on a generic rather than subject basis. Unless it becomes a designated INSET area, we do not see how the activity and practical learning methods of those teachers whom pupils rate as better teachers, and in whose lessons they learn more, can be spread more widely in order to help others expand their repertoire of teaching strategies and embrace more interactive, varied and active learning approaches with confidence.

Linked to this is the need to promote and give practical expression to the more effective transactive view of learning practices. These are clearly deserving of special grants. The issue of INSET in generic pedagogy is not confined to the technical/cognitive aspects of classroom teaching methods and activities, but embraces the task of enhancing teachers' affective or interpersonal skills. These skills were an important feature of pupils' comments on teaching and learning. A critical feature of this aspect of the transaction is communication – in all its modes. We would agree with Rives (1979) that to some extent all teachers have to be performing artists who need to make use of everyday theatrical skills, which include body actions, facial expressions, and voice modulation to convey messages and emotions, and there seems to be a clear case for training in these skills for teachers while in service.

There is also the issue of what ideology the government should be promoting in its rhetoric and climate setting generally, so as to foster more effective teaching and learning. In contrast to the messages of 'failure and under-achievement' of comprehensive school pupils and teachers, a message which many have seen government sending in recent years, there needs to be clear leadership in establishing a new ideology of achievement for the twenty-first century. This message should promulgate the belief that each pupil can achieve significant success and that all teachers can deliver the means whereby success is attained. This is not mere rhetoric, but, as we have indicated, a belief founded on the best theory and research about human intelligence and learning.

Finally, and to do with those who debate whether effective teaching can be taught, whether there is any relationship at all between the processes teacher trainees are introduced to and the product in the classroom, some have argued that there is no established connection between teaching skills and the learning outcomes of pupils. For example, Saunders (1978) suggests that the variance in pupils' achievement is well explained by other factors, such as socio-economic and ethnic status, intelligence and innate ability, so that learner differences, and not teacher differences, produce differential educational achievements. Clearly, from what we have said earlier about ideology and learner differences, we would not agree with this.

Others (e.g. Silcock 1993), while acknowledging that good teachers do make for good schools, lament the generality of advice about effective teaching which is put forward. For example, the stating of desiderata such as 'teaching well without aimlessness', 'the use of challenging questions' or 'the organization of high quality interactions' is judged as meaningless unless one can step beyond the general criteria to look at how these things are done. We would very much agree with this position, and suggest that what the teachers and pupils said about the practicalities of teaching, about what works to make good lessons in the participants' eyes, must contribute to the content of teacher training. In particular, pupils are, as we have demonstrated, very clear in their definition of good teachers and the skills associated with them, so it is time for their voice to be heard.

Issues for schools

We see three broad implications for managers in comprehensive schools arising from research findings and issues we have discussed: the need for pupils to take more responsibility for and ownership of their own learning; the need to promote a new school ideology and culture concerned with learning achievement; and, in formulating strategies for effectiveness, the need to take into account more of what teachers and pupils think about schooling.

In Chapter 2, which presented what the pupils said when asked a question about themselves as learners, they showed that overwhelmingly they hold teachers responsible for their learning, with other factors outside their immediate control taking a minor part. This construction of reality needs profound modification, since their own effort and learning strategies are also prime factors in achieved learning. Teachers know this, but we doubt whether pupils are, or have been made, sufficiently aware of their own part. By and large, as we demonstrated in Chapter 5, the cultures of learning in schools incline teachers to believe achievement is the result of endowed individual characteristics and outside social forces. The point is often made that a way of seeing the world – here the world of children's learning – is also a way of not seeing it, and there are strong grounds for arguing that other factors, such as pupil commitment and specific study skill approaches to learning, need explicit management.

A proactive approach to altering this balance would be, using Dwech's (1986) phrase, to retrain pupils' perspectives, replacing *ability* as the reason for learning failures with the notion of shortfalls of *effort* and *strategy*. Furthermore, this shift needs to be accompanied with a vigorous attack on the issue of the lack of personal individual counselling and advice *vis-à-vis* study skills. The latter is one in which some comprehensive schools are experimenting, with new policies such as study diaries and supported self-learning strategies, as we have seen for ourselves in recent years. But the research data strongly suggest a more widespread need for pupils to take

Table 8.3 Ideological perspectives contrasted

Ideology	Value position
Psychometric	A pupil's learning potential is limited by innate cognitive endowment.
Sociological	A pupil's learning potential is limited by cultural deficit from home/community background.
Transactional	Pupils' learning potential is assumed to be equal, but beginning from radically different bases of developed knowledge and understanding.

ownership of their own learning, and to achieve this we see the need for action not only at the individual interactive level, but also within the school as a whole. It is an urgent task for governors and senior managers together to establish an appropriate learning ethos in their schools.

In this respect, the senior management teams in schools will need proactively to manage the change in ideology – the set of beliefs forming a significant part of teaching staff culture – from one that eminent observers such as Hargreaves (1982) and Woods (1983) have shown to be largely based on autonomous individualism and survival strategies, to one where there are more shared beliefs about pupils learning, where there is open discussion of generic pedagogy and exchange of ideas and activities in classroom practice. In Chapter 5, we demonstrated the prevalence of 'psychological' and 'sociological' ideologies in teachers' beliefs about learning, both of which we see as now outdated. All recent research on learning and the capacity of the human brain for learning argues for the reinvention of schools' staffroom ideology as 'transactional'.

In Table 8.3, we contrast what we see to be the value positions of these ideologies in relation to the potential of pupils' learning. We use the term *transactional* ideology to embrace approaches which derive from both the *constructivist* Vygotskian view of learning and the Dwechian *incremental* view of motivation, an ideological perspective which believes that the process role of the teacher can potentially add a similar degree of gain to each individual pupil's base of knowledge and skill, while allowing that there are endowment and background variations among pupils. We are arguing, therefore, that it is a transactional ideology which should permeate school staffrooms and lead teachers' practice as they approach the twenty-first century, and that schools themselves have a key role to play in this.

We turn now to the issue of what can be learned from key participants by senior managers about their organizations. The important question here, of course, is whether pupils can make a significant contribution to the general process of evaluating the quality of what is happening. Both the teacher and pupil perspectives we discussed earlier were detailed, very perceptive and self-evidentially of value. Such perspectives are normally hidden from school managers in the helter-skelter of everyday school life, and it is not current practice for there to be a systematic collection of the views of pupils and teachers, but the quality of the information which comes from them is widely recognized. Kyriacou (1991), for example, has suggested that individual teachers 'could ask pupils to complete a questionnaire about your lessons, which explores aspects of your teaching and their experience of learning. You could interview pupils individually, or in groups, or hold a class discussion.' Clearly, on the basis of the usefulness of what the pupils said to us, we think that such practice should be encouraged, but that it should also go alongside the surveying of teacher and pupil perceptions on a systematic basis by a school's senior managers. It should be recognized that the collection of such information requires specific skills and that these research and survey skills for school managers and teachers will need to be part of INSET provision.

It is, of course, more than a matter of acquiring the appropriate tools of research. Any evaluation by pupils can carry with it an implied threat to their teachers as long as the latter maintain more traditionalist teaching ideologies, and there needs to be a recognition that the inclusion of pupils in the systematic gathering of data can of itself lead to a transformation of the process of delivering the curriculum. There is therefore a very full agenda of INSET matters.

Issues for teachers

It is not sufficiently recognized that the learning experiences teachers provide for pupils have, in recent times, been achieving more and more in terms of examination success across the ability range. The overall percentage of pupils who achieve any GCSE success (or its previous equivalent), as well as those who achieve a minimum of five good grade GCSEs, has substantially increased over the past decade. However, notwithstanding the high standard of teaching which takes place in secondary schools generally, there are some key messages for teachers from the research reported in this book. The main one is that their pupils set great store by teachers' ability to affect their learning. The clear implication from all they say about the practices of those whom they define as the 'good' teachers is that the wider adoption of 'best' practices could take pupils' learning to even higher levels of success than are achieved at the present time.

We see three broad implications for teachers from the research findings we discussed earlier: first, they need to have significantly more belief in themselves regarding the amount of difference they can make regarding pupils' learning; second, there is more room for a general shift to greater eclecticism in classroom teaching, with greater awareness and use of a wider range of activity methods, together with more open discussion of

Table 8.4 Teachers' classroom perspectives

Teacher perspective towards classroom role	Related view of pupil identity	Pupil response perspective
Reliance on survival and control (shouts at pupils)	Adversary	'Oppositional' behaviour and reluctant learner
High reliance on transmission of knowledge (talks at pupils)	Receiver of truth and wisdom	Passive learner, sometimes bored
Reliance on transaction (talks with pupils)	Co-partner in learning achievement	Co-partner and active learner, takes ownership for own learning achievement

pedagogical concepts and practice; third, there is a need to raise aware-ness of and apply interpersonal relationship strategies, to ensure a better balance between the affective and technical aspects of their teaching.

In Chapter 2, we showed that pupils believe it is teachers who make the most difference to their learning, and in Chapters 3 and 4, we gave the views of pupils on how they see the differences between good and less good teaching. The total picture is one of pupils really valuing effective teachers and believing in what teachers can help them achieve. But this contrasts with what the teachers said in Chapters 5 and 6, where they assessed the importance of their own role in pupils' learning at a very mod-est level and were also generally tentative about their teaching methods. The clear message for teachers, we reiterate, is that on the basis of what their pupils say, they need to revise their self-belief regarding the amount of difference they can and do make. Of particular relevance here, as we discussed above, is the need for a significant shift in their ideology or beliefs about children's learning potential. We suggest that the responsib-ility for effecting a shift in beliefs lies with a school's senior management.

Teachers need to have a much greater belief not only in children's learning potential but also in the extent to which they themselves can affect the learning process. From what both pupils and teachers said to us, we had a strong sense that at the present time there are three broad classroom perspectives or strategies in existence. Table 8.4 represents an initial attempt to construct a simple model derived from our analysis of the research data relating to these complex processes. We are not suggesting that the three perspectives shown have equal incidence in the real world, or that teachers' perspectives are rooted entirely within one or other of these 'ideal' typifications. Rather, there will be many mixtures. The evidence we have presented would indicate a low incidence of the 'survival and control' perspective in its pure form, and only about a quarter of teachers declared themselves to be essentially expository teachers with a transmission perspective.

In Chapters 3 and 4, we presented clear evidence that in pupils' eyes teachers need to use more devolved activity and practical teaching approaches, that they should give a significant greater weight to 'transaction' over 'transmission'. Cooper and McIntyre (1992: 213) relate *effective* teaching to a continuum of strategies, from transmission strategies to interactive and more devolved student self-directed strategies: 'some teachers appear to be able to move back and forth along this continuum, going from transmission modes through interactive modes and towards ever more student centred approaches, and back again.' Our findings corroborate the validity of this. Pupils clearly favour a plurality of teaching strategies in which there are more opportunities for them to have the space to engage in their preferred types of learning activities, something which contemporary learning theory and research says enhances explanation and effective learning. All in all, then, this important area of teachers' perspective of the classroom (i.e. of ideology and of pedagogy) needs to be brought more into open discussion by teachers.

The third clear message for teachers from the research data was that knowing what to do to foster pupils' learning involves enacting a balance between the *affective* and the *technical*, and in particular a need for more emphasis on the relationship aspects of teaching. It is clear from the pupil perspective that relationship strategies – to use Woods's (1983) term – need to be more *negotiative* in nature. What came through to us was that teacher–pupil relations are not just aspects to do with setting the social climate in the classroom, but that teachers need to see relationship techniques as teaching strategies – as of equal importance in bringing about learning.

All in all, the central message for teachers of our research findings is that the core function of the teacher's role is (as stated by Rives 1979) 'motivating or causing [learning] performance in others. If he fails to cause performance in the others, he fails to teach.' Pupils can give teachers very clear messages about how best they can achieve this good learning performance.

Implications for pupils

We have already suggested, in discussing the research findings in earlier chapters, that there is a clear implication that pupils should take more ownership of their own learning. At the present time, it is clear from their own statements that they do not 'write themselves into' the teaching and learning process sufficiently. In a way, regarding their ultimate achievement level, they are expecting too much contribution from their teachers and too little from themselves. That they need every possible relationship and pedagogic support from teachers is understandable, but this needs to

Table 8.5 Pupils' self-assessment of their
school performance ($n = 156$)

Category of response	% in category
Very good	15
Good	58
Average	26
Not very good	1
Not good at all	0

be carefully constructed so as to reveal and harness pupils' own effort, ownership and self-confidence in their own development. All that we found supports the contention of Rudduck (1996: 26) that schools and teachers should 'create time for dialogue alongside the time for teaching so that pupils begin to develop a language for thinking about learning and themselves as learners.'

The current situation may be the consequence of what we have described as the psychometric or sociological ideologies of teachers, causing pupils to think that the ultimate scope and potential of their own learning is beyond their effort and commitment. Or it may be just a matter of the lack of appropriate school-based mechanisms which can confront them about their own role in learning and can go on to challenge them to take appropriate actions.

We are aware that some schools do have counselling and schemes to support pupils' own learning, but these appear to us to be thin on the ground and of a somewhat supplementary or shadowy status, rather than existing as a main plank of a school's teaching–learning policy. Certainly, the potential is present for experimentation in enhancing pupils' ownership of their learning. In eight of the schools where we interviewed, another component of the written self-completion instrument was a question to pupils about the standard they thought they were achieving in school. In response to the statement: 'On the whole, the standard that I think I reach in school is . . .', they had to affirm one of five positions from 'very good' to 'not good at all'. The responses for 156 pupils are summarized in Table 8.5.

Almost three-quarters of the pupils thought their school performance was good or very good, and only 1 per cent thought it was below average. While we have no way of knowing how these responses would match teacher assessments of their school performance, *a priori* we think that they are based more on general impression than on the sort of data that can enter dialogue in formal reviews of progress. Formal mechanisms would allow joint definitions of 'very good' or 'not very good' etc. to be established alongside discussion of strategies for improvement.

In one school where this question was particularly relevant to the specific topic the school had chosen for us to investigate, we asked the pupils whether they thought they could improve on their declared level of performance, and, if so, how that might come about. The vast majority (92 per cent) believed they could improve. Furthermore, many of them made statements invoking their own role, and particularly with regard to improving what we would call study skills or self-organization in terms of school work and other demands in their lives.

We think, therefore, that an agenda for dialogue regarding pupils' role in their learning already exists in their own minds, ready to be 'picked up' by formal policy and mechanisms. Hence we reiterate that schools and teachers somehow need to create time for dialogue alongside the time for teaching, so that pupils begin to develop a language for thinking about learning and themselves as learners. Clearly, if it is serious about achieving optimum learning in the comprehensive schools, government also has the role of providing the resource of non-contact time, so that teachers can enact this important function.

Participant perceptions and the quality paradigm

We said in Chapter 1 that a key tenet of the *quality* or TQM is the belief that only the 'front-line' process owners can together crucially enhance quality. The research findings we have reported in this book are ample testimony that this belief is equally valid in the context of schools; that given the necessary resource of training and opportunity, it is only the teachers and pupils together who can enhance the quality of teaching and learning. Moreover, we see the findings as confirming for schools the validity of another key quality notion, that of the 'triangle of service quality' (Morgan and Murgatroyd 1994). This triangle is equilateral, with apices respectively concerned with: the interpersonal aspect of the service; the procedures or environment aspect; and the technical or professional service aspect. The model assumes a balance between the three types of input for the production of the best quality service. There seems clear evidence from our research that, for quality teaching and learning, a similar balance is required in the classroom – a balance between positive social relationships, control and order with a sense of purpose and wide-ranging teaching skills for presenting, explaining and delivering learning activities.

What this book has demonstrated is that in the search for greater effectiveness, more notice needs to be taken by those who make policy and determine the resources for schools of what teachers and pupils say. It has also evidenced that the definitions of teachers and pupils regarding classroom practices for good teaching and learning can be brought into closer harmony.

Bibliography

Babad, E., Bernieri, F., and Rosenthal, R. (1991) Students as judges of teachers' verbal and nonverbal behavior, *American Educational Research Journal*, 28, 211–34.

Bennett, N. and Dunne, E. (1994) How children learn: implications for practice, in B. Moon and A. Shelton Mayes (eds) *Teaching and Learning in the Secondary School*. London and New York: Routledge.

Bernstein, B. (1961) Social structure, language and learning, *Educational Research*, 3.

Beynon, J. (1985) *Initial Encounters in the Secondary School*. Lewes: The Falmer Press.

Bird, M. (1985) *A Study of a Community Education Project. Part 1: Organisation and Structure*. London: Inner London Education Authority.

Bruner, J. (1986) *Actual Minds, Possible Worlds*. Cambridge, MA: Harvard University Press.

Bruner, J. and Haste, H. (1987) *Making Sense*. London: Methuen.

Cooper, P. (1993) Learning from pupil perspectives, *British Journal of Special Education*, 20(4), 129–33.

Cooper, P. and McIntyre, D. (1992) Teachers' perceptions of effective classroom teaching and learning: conflicts and commonalities, Paper presented at the Annual Conference of the British Educational Research Association, Stirling University, August.

Cooper, P. and McIntyre, D. (1995) The crafts of the classroom: teachers' and students' accounts of the knowledge underpinning effective teaching and learning in classrooms, *Research Papers in Education*, 10(2), 181–216.

Cullingford, C. (1995) *The Effective Teacher*. London: Cassell.

Dwech, C. (1986) Motivational processes affecting learning, *American Psychologist*, October, 1040–8.

Eraut, M. (1997) Developing expertise in school management and teaching, in L. Kydd *et al.* (eds) *Professional Development for Educational Management*. Buckingham: Open University Press.

Gannaway, H. (1984) Making sense of school, in M. Hammersley and P. Woods (eds) *Life in School: the Sociology of Pupil Culture*. Milton Keynes: Open University Press.

Gardner, H. (1983) *Frames of Mind*. New York: Basic Books.

Gardner, H. (1994) The theory of multiple intelligences, in B. Moon and A. Shelton Mayes (eds) *Teaching and Learning in the Secondary School*. London and New York: Routledge.

Grace, G. (1984) Headteachers' judgements of teacher competence, in P. Broadfoot (ed.) *Selection, Certification and Control.* Lewes: Falmer Press.

Gray, J., Reynolds, D., Fitz-gibbon, C. and Jesson, D. (eds) (1996) *Merging Traditions: the Future of Research on School Effectiveness and School Improvement.* London: Cassell.

Hammersley, M. and Woods, P. (eds) (1984) *Life in School: the Sociology of Pupil Culture.* Milton Keynes: Open University Press.

Hargreaves, D. H. (1982) *The Challenge for Comprehensive Schools: Culture, Curriculum and Communication.* London: Routledge and Kegan Paul.

Hasting, N. (1992) Questions of motivation, *Support for Learning*, 7(3), 135–7.

Hopkins, D., Ainscow, M. and West, M. (1994) *School Improvement in an Era of Change.* London: Cassell.

Jarvis, P. (1997) Learning practical knowledge, in L. Kydd *et al.* (eds) *Professional Development for Educational Management.* Buckingham: Open University Press.

Joyce, B., Calhoun, E. and Hopkins, D. (1997) *Models of Learning – Tools for Teaching.* Buckingham: Open University Press.

Kolb, D. (1983) *Experiential Learning.* Hemel Hempstead: Prentice Hall.

Kounin, J. (1970) *Discipline and Group Management in Classrooms.* New York: Holt Rhinehart Winston.

Kyriacou, C. (1991) *Essential Teaching Skills.* Oxford: Basil Blackwell.

Lang, P. (1993) Secondary students' views on school, *Children and Society*, 7(3), 308–13.

McKelvey, J. and Kyriacou, C. (1985) Research on pupils as teacher evaluators, *Educational Studies*, 11, 25–31.

Measor, L. and Woods, P. E. (1984) *Changing Schools: Pupil Perspectives on Transfer to a Comprehensive School.* Milton Keynes: Open University Press.

Meighan, R. (1977) Pupils perceptions of the classroom techniques of postgraduate student teachers. *British Journal of Teacher Education*, 3(2), 139–48.

Mishra, S. P. (1980) Correlates of effective teaching as measured by student ratings, *Journal of Experimental Education*, 49(1), 59–62.

Moon, B. and Shelton Mayes, A. (eds) (1994) *Teaching and Learning in the Secondary School.* London and New York: Routledge.

Morgan, C. and Murgatroyd, S. (1994) *Total Quality Management in the Public Sector.* Buckingham: Open University Press.

Mumford, A. (1995) *Effective Learning.* London: Institute of Personnel and Development.

Murgatroyd, S. and Morgan, C. (1993) *Total Quality Management and the School.* Buckingham: Open University Press.

Nash, R. (1973) *Classrooms Observed.* London: Routledge and Kegan Paul.

Phelan, P., Davidson, A. L. and Cao, H. (1992) Speaking up: students' perspectives on school, *Phi Delta Kappan*, 73(9), 695–704.

Redwood, R. (1988) A recipe for staff rebellion, *The Times*, 6 February.

Reid, K., Hopkins, D. and Holly, P. (1987) *Towards the Effective School.* Oxford: Blackwell.

Reynolds, D. (ed.) (1985) *Studying School Effectiveness.* London: Falmer Press.

Rives, F. C. (1979) The teacher as a performing artist, *Contemporary Education*, 51(1), 7–9.

Roehler, L. and Duffy, G. (1986) What makes one teacher a better explainer than another, *Journal of Education for Teaching*, 12(2/3), 273–84.

Rudduck, J. (ed.) (1996) *School Improvement: What Can Pupils Tell Us?* London: David Fulton.

Saunders, J. T. (1978) Teacher effectiveness: accepting the null hypothesis, *Journal of Educational Thought*, 12(3), 184–9.

Sharp, R. and Green, A. (1975) *Education and Social Control*. London: Routledge and Kegan Paul.

Silcock, P. (1993) Can we teach effective teaching?, *Educational Review*, 45(1), 13–19.

Simon, B. (1994) Why no pedagogy in England?, in B. Moon and A. Shelton Mayes (eds) *Teaching and Learning in the Secondary School*. London and New York: Routledge.

Smith, B. (1989) Preparing to leave school in the 1990s, *Pastoral Care*, June, 6–12.

Soo Hoo, S. (1993) Students as partners in research and restructuring schools, *The Educational Forum*, 57, 386–94.

Vygotsky, L. S. (1978) *Mind and Society: the Development of Higher Psychological Processes*. Cambridge, MA: Harvard University Press.

Wehlage, G. G., Rutter, E. A., Gregory, A., Smith, N. L. and Fernandez, R. R. (1989) *Reducing the Risk: Schools as Communities of Support*. Lewes: Falmer Press.

Woods, P. (1979) *The Divided School*. London: Routledge and Kegan Paul.

Woods, P. (1983) *Sociology and the School*. London: Routledge and Kegan Paul.

Woods, P. (1996) *Researching the Art of Teaching*. London and New York: Routledge.

Wragg, E. C. (ed.) (1984) *Classroom Teaching Skills*. London: Croom Helm.

Index

MODELS OF LEARNING – TOOLS FOR TEACHING

Bruce Joyce, Emily Calhoun and David Hopkins

Learning experiences are composed of content, process and social climate. As teachers, we create for and with our children opportunities to explore and build important areas of knowledge, develop powerful tools for learning, and live in humanizing social conditions.

The purpose of this book is to introduce some of the array of models of teaching that have been developed, polished and studied over the last twenty-five years. It is hoped that teachers, advisers, inspectors, teacher educators and educational researchers will study these models. If they do, they will discover elegant modes of teaching that have great power for learners. Some of these models have been shown both to accelerate rates of learning and also bring within reach of pupils types of conceptual control and modes of inquiry which have been almost impossible to generate through traditional chalk and talk teaching. Rather than being formulas to be followed slavishly, each model brings teachers into the study of how students learn thereby promoting reflective action research in the classroom.

Contents

224pp   0 335 19990 9 (Paperback)

TOTAL QUALITY MANAGEMENT AND THE SCHOOL

Stephen Murgatroyd and Colin Morgan

The management team within the school are currently faced with a great deal of pressure to achieve a range of 'performance' expectations in a climate of increasing uncertainty, financial stringency and competition. Total Quality Management is a framework and set of practical resources for managing organizations in the 1990s. Based on sound principles and a strong body of experience, Total Quality Management provides a school based management team with the tools they need to become highly effective in meeting the goals of their stakeholders, and in creating a place that teachers want to work in.

This book is the first to fully examine the practice of Total Quality Management in the context of schooling. It looks, for instance, at the nature of a school's strategic management in the context of growing competition and expectations for performance; and at the positioning of the school in terms of vision and mission. It considers the setting of 'outrageous' or exceptional goals to create momentum and alignment and explores the nature of high performing teams within the school. It discusses commitment-building as part of the new quality culture and involving stakeholders in the daily management of the school.

It is practical and well-illustrated with case vignettes and examples of Total Quality Management in action. It is based on the experience of two senior academic practitioners who have both carried out extensive work in school management and development.

Contents
Making sense of schooling in the 1990s – Choosing a generic strategy – Definitions of quality and their implications for TQM in schools – A model for TQM in the school – Vision, ownership and commitment – Customers and processes as the basis for schooling – Outrageous goals and the task of continuous improvement – Teams, team performance and TQM – Daily management tools for effective TQM – Implementing TQM in the school – Postscript – References – Index.

240pp   0 335 15722 X (Paperback)

TEACHER RESEARCH AND SCHOOL IMPROVEMENT
OPENING DOORS FROM THE INSIDE

Rob Halsall (ed.)

This book is about the key role the teaching profession itself has to play in school effectiveness and improvement. The contributors argue that for genuine school improvement, strategies and approaches must evolve from teachers themselves. Dictates mandated from 'on high' simply will not work. Any approach to school improvement must recognize the complex nature of teachers' work, the importance of flexibility and the need for on-going learning to cope with a system marked by unpredictability. Drawing together insights from the school improvement literature, this book argues strongly for teacher research as a central strategy in improving schools and provides illuminating case studies of teacher research for school improvement at whole school, department and classroom levels. The book offers stimulating reading for education managers, classroom teachers and teacher researchers in both primary and secondary schools.

Contents

Part 1: The case for teacher research as a strategy for school improvement – School effectiveness and school improvement: meanings and traditions – School improvement: an overview of key findings and messages – Innovation and inertia – Teacher research for school improvement – Part 2: Case studies of teacher research for school improvement – Action research for improving educational practice – Getting the measure of bullying – 52 absentees: a case study of one school's attempt to improve attendance – 'No problem here': action research against racism in a mainly white area – Researching knowledge of, and communicating about student progress: a case study of collaborative research – Using structured play to promote language development in the early years – Monitoring students' work to raise attainment and investigate the problem of underachievement – Developing literacy – Part 3: Teacher research, professionalism and teacher development – The case studies discussed – Teacher professionalism, teacher development and school improvement – References – Index.

Contributors

Michael Bassey, Kevin Brain, Karen Carter, Mike Cockett, Mary Connery, Patricia Donald, Susan Gosling, Jan Green, Rob Halsall, Jean Hamilton, Karen Hanks, Jill Richford, Rosemary Rodger, Ian Stronach, Tim Whitwell.

240pp   0 335 19952 6 (Paperback)   0 335 19953 4 (Hardback)